Flipping Keys

Self-Made Real Estate King

Cesar Piña

IKONIC
Books

Flipping Keys

Self-Made Real Estate King

© 2021 by Cesar Piña

Printed in the United States of America.

ISBN-13: 978-0-578-84776-4

Cover photo by Felix Natal, Jr

IKONIC BOOKS

Newark, NJ

What people are saying about Cesar Piña:

Yall need to join this team with Jen and Flippin_NJ. They got the strongest team in the real estate game. Get in where you fit in. Teamwork make a dream work. **- Snoop Dogg**

I was thinking wouldn't it be great to see @flipping_nj and @djenvy on TV, so you can understand the real estate business. Done deal! **- 50 Cent**

He owns damn near half of Jersey. He's gonna be the first Dominican Donald Trump in the real estate business. **- N.O.R.E**

The definition of "self-made," Piña got his start investing in rental buildings in New Jersey, and from there expanded to New York City, Miami and Chicago. Today, he is worth an estimated $65 million dollars and owns more than 1,100 rental units nationwide.
- Miami Agent Magazine

Cesar Piña is a successful real estate mogul. His road to real estate is not your typical story. Being a natural hustler, he has been able to transform his skill into the corporate world. With that skill and hard work, he has had some incredible accomplishments like being able to provide for his family, being able to employ an amazing team, and helping to revitalize neighborhoods. **- ED Times Youth Blog**

I dedicate this book to my wife Jennifer,
my daughter, Taylor, my brother Luchi,
and my parents. I love you all.

TABLE OF CONTENTS

Introduction

I never thought I would "make it", but now when I wake up, it really feels like I'm living the dream. I never envisioned this, what I've termed as *"from start to flip"* wasn't even in my vocabulary. Everything that I enjoy today is unbelievable. If it hadn't had been for the radical change in my ways, I'd probably still be locked up in prison or unfortunately lying six feet under, dead . . . believe me.

Most people consider me to be lucky, but this has nothing to do with luck. I sit here looking into my past and I realize that despite how uneasy it is to relive some of these moments, they are all part of a jigsaw puzzle. Only now that every piece has came together, I see how they have created a pretty awesome story. There's no way I'd be here telling you this story if it were not for each and every piece.

Most things happen for a reason. The good, the bad, and the ugly things. I'm here to share some of my, what most people would call "bad moments" so that you can see how I was able to turn them around. They all led up to some of my "greatest moments." They all led up to the successful life I live now. I made the best out of the most ugly situations a man can go through. I share my past, so that you can be inspired to push through your most challenging times too. It may be difficult now, but don't take the hard times for granted. They can all become blessings, when you change your mindset and the way you think about them. You do have the ability to turn your life around. I am here as a living proof, that it CAN be done.

Throughout my life, I have always found myself in some of the craziest of situations. Situations that left me confused and wondering, why do these things always happen to me? Why me? As a young kid growing up, none of it made any sense. No matter what I tried to do, somehow, matters just got worse. Despite the somewhat bizarre stories in my youth. I have always tried to live a moral life. I come from a solid home where I was raised by both Mom and Dad. I think my strong family values were instilled from such a young age by my parents, that they couldn't help but become such a big part of me. My parents still remain together to this day, family and loyalty is everything. Even though my parents were always supportive, and I came from a solid home, once I became a teenager, I wanted to be independent, and free. I no longer wanted to view them as a crutch for anything I needed. I wanted to provide for myself, and them. It seems that from a very young age, I wanted to be my own boss. The overall adventure of the great unknown of life itself, and making my own money consumed me.

Some people think my success was just handed to me and I was made overnight. Nothing about those statements are true, they actually couldn't be farthest away from any type of reality for me. It's been a long and steady grind, and more importantly it's been hard work. Nothing was easy, nothing still is. New levels of success provide new challenges.

There are days when I sit around reminiscing about my crazy past and consider myself extremely fortunate. Not lucky. I consider myself fortunate, and blessed, to have survived my youth. I wasn't lucky because it took a lot of hard work. Many who have been in the same predicament as me, couldn't and still haven't survived or thrived, so it has nothing to do with luck. I've been a witness to so many things throughout my life and I could've easily been the suspect or the victim of them. Yet, for some reason, God always seemed to have had a bigger and better plan for me. I didn't know it at the time, but someone upstairs was watching over me because I've lost count with the amount of close calls and run-ins I've had. I made the most of my chances and turned them around.

Today, my life is a complete flip! Pun absolutely intended. People see the smile on my face, the clothes I wear, or even the celebrities I call friends, and think they know the whole story. But it's the back story of my life that nobody sees, that's where the gold is, and that's what I'm trying to share in this book. The crowds will never see behind the scenes, where I was alone and afraid. They only see the confident 'Real Estate King'. It's been a tough road to get to where I am, and like with so many similar stories, I have had my fair share of tears, fears and solitude. I've had many dark sleepless nights wondering what the heck will come of tomorrow. There's been so many times when I didn't have the money, and I didn't have the answers. If you're going through the same thing, believe me, I've been there, and I know exactly what you're going through. I found a way out, and maybe my road can provide another path for you.

In High School, I did the bare minimum just to get by. It wasn't that I wasn't smart or didn't take school seriously, I just didn't find any motivation in school. I saw no value in school, and my dream reached far beyond getting into college. It didn't really help that my Dad would make not so subtle comments about, big dreams and big houses. School never felt right for me. It just seemed like Real Estate was being branded in my psyche instead of college. I remember the days when my Dad would drive my brother and I around the posh neighborhoods when we were kids. He would point at houses and claim them, saying that if he ever hit the jackpot and won the lottery he would buy each one. I loved when he would do that, because I would visualize it actually happening. I would see myself in a big fancy house with a huge pool in the backyard. I saw the vision so many times, it's like it had already become a memory. It appears my Dad was laying out clues about my destiny of buying multiple properties from day one.

My dad actually came close to winning the lottery one day, but it was nowhere near what it would cost to buy his dream home. I laugh about it now, but I still remember breaking down, because I really thought we were finally able to afford the one $400,000 house we had all fallen in love with. We knew it as "La Casa Coñazo". I was so let down when I saw that $20,000 was in no way enough money to purchase it, but the disappointment planted a silent motivation inside of me. My Dad's dream of buying a $400,000 house became my new dream, without knowing it. I was crushed, but it was one of those moments in my youth that I promised myself to focus and be determined to make it in life, no matter what I had to do. My main goal was just to make a lot of money.

Although there were no serious thoughts of me getting into real estate at the time, I do believe that my Dad driving us around and pointing at nice houses is what sparked those thoughts and ideas of me getting into the business myself in the future. Besides showing houses on rides in his car, my Dad was also a dreamer. Before zillow.com and instant listings on your phone my Dad figured out how to research the housing market and seek out for home values. He would park in front of some of the houses he liked and call the numbers on the for-sale signs. The phone calls still make me laugh to this day, because he would say something like,

"Hi, this is Michael, I own five restaurants in the area and I am looking at the house on Atlantic. This house is EXACTLY WHAT I'M LOOKING FOR, can you tell me more about it?"

My brother and I would crack up in the backseat at the charade my dad would pull, knowing damn well he couldn't afford any of those houses.

Failure has also been an important part of my life and ultimately my formation, it took me failing over and over again, which includes doing some prison time to finally get my life on the right track. Losses took a toll on me, life almost got me to the point where I wanted to give up, but for whatever reason, many people around me would tell me that I was a better person than the one I was being, and to give up the act. I probably should have listened, but I didn't. As I look back, I can't deny my awkward past, but I've learned from it, and I've moved on. I think it's safe to say that for everyone, you can't change your past, but what you can do is bounce back and grow. That's where I find myself today. No matter how hard times get, I've learned this tough lesson throughout my life. So again, I must state for the record, where I am at today never came to me easy.

Most people only see illusions of *"making it,"* and just staying at the top, once you've got there. I always envisioned myself not just talking about it but seeing the vision become a reality. I always believed that no matter whatever came my way, I could achieve this dream, no matter how far it seemed to be. Although I have made it this far, my motivation has compelled me to go harder and further. But with this determination and pursuit, the decision to cut many people off has also been necessary. Many obstacles tried to dissuade me from continuing, but I had to overcome these issues and disconnect myself from many people so that a clear vision of where I wanted to be could exist without any distractions. The hip-hop artist Notorious B.I.G famously rapped *"more money, more problems"*, but to me, it doesn't have to be that way, with more money comes more opportunities seize the the problems and flip them.

I've been on a mission. I've tried to tell my story to thousands so that when it's told you can envision yourself in my story, and see how everyone can achieve greatness. One of the many things that I've learned on my way is to never allow anyone or anything to derail you off your track, stay focused. I was always willing to try and try again no matter how many times I was turned down or ignored. No one could feel or understand my struggle. But most importantly, no one was going to stop me. It wasn't long before I began to see how some of the people I considered the closest to me, began to look and act differently towards me when I choose to better myself. Unfortunately, the majority of people who don't like it when you are doing well, are the ones to condemn you later on and tell you *"never forget where you came from"*, as if I had. I never did and I never will. I do remember those who supported me from the very beginning. From day one, were my immediate family. My ride wasn't always a smooth one. At times, it was very rocky and bumpy. But as fate would have it, no matter what got in my way, I went through it, learned from it and tried not to look back in regret.

My vision is clear, and I hope it will be for you as well. I saw the end from the beginning. I'm now walking a path that I felt I was destined for. I've been through both the ups and downs throughout my life, but I was determined to keep my wins this time. There has been no turning back once I saw the fruits of the labor, sweat, and hard work. Most people fold and give up when they are at their lowest point in life, don't be like them, I chose not to and because of that, I made the turn, and success has greeted me. The same can be for everyone. Some look at the cards they have been dealt, and fold. As for me, my hardest times became my greatest blessing. It's by looking at life like that, that will give you an advantage. Deep inside, I knew that I was going to be somebody and destiny was at my fingertips but I didn't know how things were going to turn around. Life did a turn around and this is how my life turned full circle.

"Never pay retail for anything."

Memory Lane

I was born at Roosevelt Hospital, Manhattan New York, June 4, 1978. At that time, we lived in Washington Heights. As soon as kindergarten ended, my parents decided to send me to live in Santo Domingo in the Dominican Republic with my grandparents. I stayed with them during the school year and then spent the summer back at home in New York with my parents. I did that until I was in fifth grade before moving back for good with my parents. I was just 10 years old. My grandfather Ito and my grandmother Ita took really good care of me. Those were our nicknames for them, I couldn't say the words Abuelito or Abuelita meaning Grandpa or Grandma, so Ito and Ita they became. I had a really awesome childhood. My grandparents always made sure that I felt loved. Out of all their grandchildren, it has been said that I was always their favorite.

My grandparents always made sure that I always felt loved by them. On my 7th birthday, they threw me a big party. They went all out for me and they did with the intention of me feeling at home since I was away from the United States. They didn't want me to feel left out or that my parents had abandoned me, so at that very early age, I was showered with a whole lot of gifts, and even ended up having my picture in the local newspaper. I still recall the Rooster I got as a gift as well, my grandfather took that same rooster and put him in cockfights. It's so interesting how my memories at that age highlight the funniest stories.

Being big boned runs in my family. My grandfather stood about 6'4 and weighed 320lbs. To us he was our gentle giant. He would always greet and shake hands with people even when they were total strangers. Just like he tried to do one day while he and I were on our way to get the mail. While visiting New York City one summer, I remember us walking towards the mailbox when a man looking very suspicious came walking towards us. My grandfather tried greeting the man as he got closer to us. This man must have thought my grandfather was a pushover just because he was older, but he soon found out that Grandpa Ito was not the kind of man who would back down to anyone. The man walked up to my grandfather and tried to rob him while acting like he had a gun under his t-shirt. My grandfather, without hesitation, turned and elbowed the man in the face, the man took off running. My grandfather looked at me afterwards with a straight face and asked,

"Why didn't you bite him after I hit him?"

He started laughing and saw me standing there confused about what had just occurred.

Looking back now as an adult, I am really happy and fortunate that I got to spend the little time that I did with them when I was a kid. In fact, it was probably the only real time that I was able to enjoy the years of my youth. On September 4th, 1989 I moved back home to New York with my parents. The day I was leaving the Dominican Republic for good, my grandfather told me that it would be the last time that I would see him alive. Unfortunately, he was right. Two weeks later, on September 19th, he passed away. I was heartbroken. My love for my grandfather ran and still runs very deep. He was a positive influence in my childhood, and that continues into my adult years.

To this day, I still speak to my grandmother at least twice a day. In fact, she's the only person that I know today that always asks me if I ever need anything when almost everyone around me expects a handout. Once I became successful, I started questioning those who hung around me. Why do they want to be near me? Was it the money? Was it the fame? It's never been like that with Ita. She has taught me what real love is. Not a love because of what I have done or what I have, but an unconditional love that sees me for me. She taught me what it's like to be loved, with the purest of motives. The best kind of love. My Ita is 100 years old as I write this book today, and still loves and treats me like she did when I was a kid. It was great to live in the Dominican Republic with them both.

When I came back home to New York, what I saw in Washington Heights opened my eyes. Things were much different from what I had gotten used to back in the Dominican Republic. We're talking about the 80s and 90s, when almost every block was surrounded by drugs. I used to see all the drug dealers driving around in nice cars, wearing fancy jewelry, showcasing the pretty girls, and flashing everything else that came with the lifestyle that drug dealing boasts. At that point, I was in the 6th grade. I was still crushed about my grandfather's passing and it hit me pretty hard because Ito and Ita had always been there with me since I could remember.

Moving back home with my parents had a big impact on the way that I began to live my life. I began adjusting quickly to the environment around me. It wasn't long before I began to act out and misbehave. I could feel myself changing almost overnight. Before you knew it, me and my brother started running with the wrong crowd. I see the same scenario with young people today. I felt like we had to dive right in. We went from being kids running around playing games to being *lookouts* for the neighborhood drug dealers. We started making a few dollars here and there, hanging out later and later in the night, and just like that, the life as a hustler came to me from the streets.

My dad was an alcoholic at that time. He would work hard all week and then get drunk on the weekends. This was perfect for us because it gave us more time to stay out. But to be clear, my parents did the best they could for us with the resources they could afford, but when weekends came around my dad would always binge drink. For some reason, he would feel extra adventurous off the liquor, and just like that, he would go grab one of his guns and start playing around with it. My dad would even go outside and just start shooting bullets into the nights sky.

On Sunday's though, things were a little different. Sunday was family day. It was the one day that we would all get together and enjoy spending some time with each other. My Dad would go to the shop and return with roses for my Mum. Then, we would all walk from our house to go and eat at the Chinese restaurant two blocks down the street. It was one of my favorite days of the week. My parents always made sure that we dressed up when we went out together. Everything was picture perfect. We were like the ideal Hispanic American family. We usually stayed at the restaurant for about two hours eating and then talking about how our week went.

My dad's drinking day stories could go on forever, but the funniest ones to me, was when I would walk into the room where he had been drinking and found him passed out drunk. Back in the day, we used to have this old school record player at home and every time that he would start feeling good off the liquor, he would play it really loud. In fact, so loud that you could even hear it from outside the house. He would always play his favorite song *Tabaco y Ron* by Fernandito Villalona. Once all you heard was the record skipping ♫ *Tobacco,* ♫ *Tobacco,* ♫ *Tobacco,* ♫ *Tobacco,* that's when you knew the night was over for him and that he had fallen asleep.

Another crazy moment I can share about my dad's drinking came in the summer of 1990. It was around the time when I was going into the 8th grade. I was in the living room watching *In Living Color* while my dad was on the couch getting drunk. There was really nothing unusual about him going to grab one of his guns once he got drunk. I was already used to it. But on this day, I remember sitting right in front of him as I watched the show on television. Next thing you know, the gun goes off! The bullet goes flying right past me, nearly hitting me on my right shoulder and making a hole in the wall. Of course, it wasn't on purpose. Somehow, my dad ended up cutting his finger after the bullet had been shot. My dad was bleeding like crazy. My mom came running in to see what had occurred and noticed all the blood on my dad's hands while he was still holding onto the gun. My dad's hand was hurting him so much that he started running towards the door to go to the hospital. My mom, thinking that he was actually chasing after her as he ran towards the door, began yelling out loud *"Oh my god he's going to kill me!"* and ran the opposite way.

Later that night, the cops came to our house to investigate what had occurred. Back then, the cops didn't really care to follow up on anything unless someone had been shot or killed. They came in, looked around for a few minutes and just saw kids playing around and left. My dad was never charged with any crime. That was the incident that scared him straight. One shot, one near miss, one moment in our lives changed everything. That day back in 1990 was the last time my dad ever had alcohol, he has been sober ever since.

A couple of weeks after the gun incident, we ended up moving out of New York and went to live in Clifton, New Jersey. My parents were still a little worried that the police would come back and arrest my dad over the gun incident. Other than that, I believe that my parents really just wanted to give us a better life than the one we were living in Washington Heights. But as we all know, Paterson is not that different from any other city in New York. No matter how hard they tried to keep us from getting into trouble, my brother and I still ended up choosing the street life instead.

"Leverage your money."

Young Hustler

Once we settled in Clifton, I quickly made new friends. We ran the streets and did all of the typical things that teenagers did back in those days. We had a lot of fun. Of course, not everything that we did was all positive, but it gave me a sense of belonging. I was always a good kid. But for some reason, I was drawn to the shady side of the streets. The obsession was not because I wanted to be a criminal but because it seemed entertaining, adventurous and just alive to me. I was always intrigued and fascinated by the things I saw every day. Despite being in New Jersey, it seemed like Paterson was no different to New York City.

Not even a year after moving to New Jersey, I ended up catching my first charge as a juvenile when I was thirteen. The charges were for vandalism. It wasn't really anything serious. My friends and I were all just running around spraying graffiti on any free wall we could find. But because of this nonsense, I was placed in a youth house for almost three weeks and ended up on probation for the charge. My parents weren't really all that upset with me. It was only graffiti to them and it wasn't technically all that big of a deal. Unlike any other normal kid who would feel troubled and discouraged after being arrested for the first time, I felt like I'd arrived. Once I completed my time at the youth house, it didn't take long for me to get right back to hanging out with my friends in the streets and picking up even worse habits.

As I look back, me being an entrepreneur and a businessman began in formation by the hustle that came offered to me in the streets. A hustle that came to me from the inability to do anything else. I compared the way that we lived to others, and noticed the difference between what they had and what I wanted. Why did others have it better than me? Why couldn't I have what they had? I never felt like the street life was robbing me of my childhood, but the way that I was living, I didn't really care about doing the things that normal teenagers were doing anymore. I wasn't into sports and I most definitely didn't care about being an honor roll student. All I cared about was making my own choices in life and succeeding.

After living at our house in Paterson for ten years, the landlord decided to sell the house. We had to move all over again. I remember it all as if it were yesterday. This is when real estate taught me a lesson. I was in my bedroom and I heard someone knocking on our door. My dad, who had been sitting in the living room, got up and answered it. Once he opened the door, I saw the landlord. At first, I thought that we had done something wrong when he asked if he could come in so they could talk. However, once they sat down and began to talk, I noticed that the landlord was explaining to my dad that he wanted to sell the house. Although I was very disappointed, the situation behind the decision to sell the house actually became one of the first lessons that I had learned regarding buying and selling a house.

The landlord was sitting at our table when he opened up his folder filled with all types of documents. Inside the folder were the receipts from all the rent payments that my parents had made throughout the ten years that we had been living there. The landlord explained in just a few sentences that the amount of rent that we had paid added up to the full amount for him to pay the house off. I knew then that I never wanted to be in that type of predicament in my life. This was a pivotal moment in my life and it became one of the first lessons I learned when it came to real estate. The landlord ended up selling the house and we ended up moving to Clifton.

After the move, that fire in me motivated me to pursue a new hustle, flipping clothes. I found a flea market called the Meadowlands Flea Market. They had bootleg items that claimed to be brand name but were actually knockoffs. I would buy them at Meadowlands at the reduced price and then turn around and sell them for double or sometimes even triple the price. One of the main things that I would always purchase would be fake Polo sweatshirts that I would buy for ten dollars and then turn around and sell for thirty dollars on the street. I was always hustling something and making profits any way I could. My mind was sharp and I was always coming up with new ways to make a living even though I was still in high school. It felt good to be somewhat financially independent and afford anything I wanted.

The more money I made, the more I wanted to make, whether legal or not. That's a big problem. I sometimes wonder how many young people are talented enough to be entrepreneurs in many things, but find themselves with just one option and turn to a life of crime. Not good. The hustle became sort of like an addiction for me. By my sophomore year, my hustling evolved to drugs. I began selling marijuana, or as we all still know it as weed. Everyone was into smoking it back then. I made a killing off it. I sold weed the entire time I was in high school. Things really got crazy by the time I reached my senior year. I was *the man* back then. I began hanging out and partying a lot more. I was constantly around drugs and always making money. To be honest, I began to care less about school and focused more on looking good and making money.

Around the time I was supposed to graduate, my counselor called me into his office to let me know that I was apparently going to be one credit short from getting my diploma. Although I really didn't care about school as much as I should have, I didn't want to end up staying back either. Somehow, when I transferred to my new high school in Clifton, I lost credit because of absences. I was absent too many times. The counselor at the time didn't know who it was that had written the letter, so he sent me to go and check with all of my teachers to see who it was that had written it. We were unable to figure out

I'm grateful to the many people who believed in me as a young man with no direction, and had grace for me to help me get through the moments where I needed a break in life.

which teacher it was, so the counselor just decided to rip up the letter and allowed me to graduate. My counselor Lou Fraulo did me that one favor and to this day I'll never forget it. I remember him telling me in his office that if I ever saw him in public to just say hi to him. About two years later, I ended up seeing him out and about and ended up giving him a big bear hug instead. I'm grateful to the many people who believed in me as a young man with no direction, and had grace for me to help me get through the moments where I needed a break in life. Mr. Fraulo is one of them and I'll never forget it.

I really didn't have any plans after I graduated from high school. Some of my friends had joined the Marines, so I thought maybe that would be a great idea for me to pursue. In my mind, I felt like I needed to do something once the reality sunk in that I was no longer in school anymore and that I had to go out into the real world and be a man. I figured, why not give it a shot? I even made an appointment to meet with a recruiter the following weekend. Temporarily, I felt really confident about my decision to join the military. But apparently, life had other plans for me. A few days before I was supposed to meet with the recruiter, I ended up catching another charge, but this time it was for marijuana.

I just had gotten home from getting a haircut when two guys came up to me and asked me for a few bags of weed. After getting what they wanted, they went along down the street. Tone and I started getting high ourselves and while we sat there passing the blunt back and forth, I saw the cops coming our way. Come to find out, the two guys that had bought the weed from me got caught and ended up telling the police where they had got the weed from. The cops went overboard. As soon as they searched me and found me in possession of marijuana, they handcuffed me and began to threaten me by saying they were going to arrest my parents and get them deported. Yeah right!

The charge wasn't serious, but it was enough for the Marines to no longer be able to recruit me. After that, I just said *fuck it* and got really heavy into the drug game. I began hearing about a few spots in Harlem, so I started making my way down to 125th on Lenox Ave and began purchasing pounds of weed from my new Jamaican "connect" named Scarface. He really had a scar on his face too. He told me that he had gotten slashed in the face back in Kingston. I remember the first time I walked into his studio apartment where there were garbage bags filled to the top with marijuana. It was crazy.

After picking up my weed, I would bring it all right back to Jersey to bag it up and hit the streets to make money. At that time, I used to get a pound of weed for about $600 and I'd bag up the weed into five nickel bags. A nice profit of $2000 per pound. That was a lot of money back in the 90s. I was flipping about four to five pounds a week. You can say I was killing it. I could afford anything that I wanted at the time. Ironically, when I would ride down to Harlem to re-up on weed, I would look around and see all the Brownstones that were boarded up and being sold for just a dollar. There were blocks upon blocks filled with those vacant Brownstones. I never thought about it then, but now those brownstones are worth about 4 million dollars today.

Although I sometimes ran across the thought of wanting to do better in life, it made it harder for me to do anything other than what I was doing. I was making a ton of money. By the time I was nineteen, I was averaging close to $10,000 a week in pure profit. Pure untaxable cash profit. The only issue was that I wasn't saving a single dollar of it. I look back now and wonder how could I just blow through all that cash. Looking at it now I see how so many people aren't lacking the finances for opportunities, they're just squandering opportunities, but with a little guidance they could make a killing if directed right. I was blowing money on anything and everything. I probably wouldn't have even been able to afford bail had I been caught. But that was the life of the typical street hustler. We ran through our money just as fast as we made it. As long as we were making it all back, we didn't have a care in the world about saving any of it.

Most of us never really cared or took the time to understand the risks that we were taking while out in the streets selling drugs. Most of us had to find out the hard way. I found out when I ended up catching yet another case for marijuana possession. This time, the situation was a lot different from the charge I had before. This arrest gave me an inside look into how our system is set up though. It's a corrupt system, designed for most of us to fail and to trap as many of us as possible.

I ended up getting caught yet again for possession of marijuana right down the street from my house, only this time it was a lot more serious. When the cops jumped out from their cruisers, they immediately surrounded me and began searching me. They had jumped out so fast that I didn't even have the opportunity to try to run. This time they got me with 190 nickel bags of marijuana. Although it sounds like I had been caught with a lot on me, it was only a street worth of $950. But it wasn't how much I had been caught with that was the issue. It was where I got caught that was the bigger problem.

I never really understood anything about being arrested other than just being charged, bailing out, or doing time for it. The crazy thing was that at the time that I had been arrested, I happened to be standing between a park, a firehouse, and a school. All three of these zones were right there on our street. So, for each one of those zones it was a different charge. Each one was a charge for selling drugs within a few feet of all of those locations. On one arrest, I had three different marijuana charges. You would have thought I had been caught with a kilo of cocaine the way that they were trying to prosecute me for it.

My parents hired an attorney for the case. Back then there was this judge in Clifton that everyone called Hanging Harry. He was known for sentencing people to the max regardless of the charges they came into his courtroom with. I remember turning to my attorney on my first day in court and asking him,

"So, what's the worst that I'm looking at for my charges?"

With a straight face he turned to me and said,

"You're looking at about fifteen years maximum."

I looked at him and said,

"It was fuckin weed, what the fuck you mean fifteen years! Are you serious?"

I immediately felt like I was about to cry. Here I am, just graduating high school, starting my life and now I'm facing all that time in prison and for weed of all things. For garbage weed at that, because it wasn't even top of the line shit.

I stood in front of the judge and he ends up giving me this ridiculous bail of $70,000. It was crazy. I've seen people get lower bonds for more serious crimes than what I had been charged with. But as ridiculous as that was, I felt like it was also a blessing because little did I know, I later found out that they had been surveilling my house for weeks. Although I never kept any drugs in my house, I had rented an apartment just down the street where I would keep my stash at. Because if there's one main rule that most people should really follow, it's to never ever keep the drugs where you sleep at night.

I'm really not sure if while the police were watching me, that they were also watching me going in and out of the stash house too. But if they were, they probably would not have found anything there. Fortunately enough for me, it just so happened that the weekend before I was arrested, someone had broken into my stash house and stole the safe where I kept all of my drugs. To this day, I still haven't found out who went to my stash house and robbed me. But whoever it was, got me really good.

In that safe, I had my money, a couple of pounds of weed, a few ounces of cocaine and even had a dirty loaded illegal .38 special that I had purchased in the street. Had they raided my stash house instead of catching me in the streets, my situation would have been a lot worse. I probably would have been looking at more than the 15 years they were already trying to hang me with. Looking back, I must say those breaks I caught really allowed me to live a successful life today. I'm blessed, no doubt about it.

Once they figured out that I wasn't going to be able to make bail, they sent me down to a holding cell where other inmates had been waiting to get called into the courtroom. While sitting in the holding cell stressing out in silence, I looked outside through a small window and noticed that it was raining. A few minutes later, I heard a young lady's voice coming from another cell singing

"♫ *I saw you and him, walking in the rain, you were holding hands and I will never be the same*" ♫.

On the other end, I heard another inmate rapping the part that followed those lyrics. I couldn't understand it. There I was stressing the fuck out that I'm about to go to prison to do time with the *big boys* and these two fools are just singing as if they didn't have a care in the world.

The next morning, the officers came through yelling and waking us all up. The girl down the hall that had been singing the night before was now screaming at the officers. She was just going in on them bright and early.

"*Fuck you officer, let me out of this cell and I will fuck you up*" she kept hollering.

In my mind I'm thinking, that girl is tough as shit. The officers came down cell by cell to take us out and chained us all up together in one row. I was nervous as hell and wasn't really paying attention to anything. Once I was chained up, I looked up to my right and noticed that the girl had long hair, painted nails and... a fucking full grown out beard! She was a fucking dude! She was a transexual. She was pretty big too. All I kept thinking to myself was, damn, she could probably fuck, me, up! But once we started talking to each other about our situations, she ended up being cool as hell with me.

I explained everything to her about my case and how they were trying to hang me. Having had so much experience when it came to doing time, she told me that my case was bullshit and that once I made it to superior court that my bail was going to be dropped, and that I would probably only be looking at a nine month sentence. She said that my bail wasn't going to be nowhere near the $70,000 that they had set prior. She went on to tell me that the only asshole judges that would do people like that, are judges like Hanging Harry in Clifton. A few hours later, she absolutely was right. They did exactly what she said they would do.

After seeing the judge, I was taken to Passaic County Jail where they held me in a holding cell until they were able to figure out the unit where I was going to be sent to start doing my time. While in holding, as if I hadn't been through enough already, the guard brings in this African American dude who was about 6'4 and weighed about 350lbs. I was eighteen years old and weighed about 140lbs. The other inmates that were being held in the cell along with me were no bigger or much older than I was. The inmate that they had just brought in had sniffed like a half a gram of heroin. He was so high that his eyes were closed and his neck was so weak that he could barely keep his head straight.

There was a lot of space for him to just pick a spot and sit or lay down. Instead, he took about two steps in and stood right in the middle of our holding cell and fell asleep standing up. A few seconds later, he drops straight to the floor and ends up busting his head open after hitting the concrete. There was blood everywhere. We all just looked at him like this fucking guy is crazy! A few minutes later, he stands back up, falls asleep again, and then falls right back on the concrete and busts his head open again. He did that at least four or five times. The guards never even bothered to come and see what had been going on in our cell. We were all petrified and just looking at each other. I remember whispering to one of them,

"We're all in here together, if he comes after any of us, we have to stick together and beat his ass up."

We were all freaked the fuck out by that dude.

My first real prison experience was crazy from the start. All I kept thinking to myself was that they were going to end up killing me in there. It was a hell of an experience, and those were just my first few days there. I was so shook up that I couldn't even use the bathroom. I was scared shitless. *Literally*. The heroin sniffer was high for about four days straight. I still remember when the guards would come around to do a count with their K-9 and they would put the dog right up to that man's face while barking, and he never even woke up. He was so high that when he finally came down from it and opened up his eyes, he didn't even know where he was at, or why he was in prison.

Finally, I was able to make it to superior court and they ended up granting me my bail. Everything happened exactly how the *"the singing girl"* back in the holding cell had told me. The judge dropped my bail to $25,000 and I was released. That *"girl"* did a better job preparing me for court proceedings and sentencing than my own attorney. I ended up getting sentenced to nine months in jail for possession of marijuana. Although I had just dodged doing fifteen years, and you might think that would have slowed me down. It didn't. I was blinded by foolishness, not taking the break of not doing serious time in prison, I continued. But the silver lining in the next phase of my life was Jen, my future wife.

"Always partner up, not down."

My Ride or Die

I met Jen in 1998. Playing spades over at my friend's house, I saw my future wife. I was twenty years old at the time and fresh out of jail. My friend had a garage at his house in Clifton where we all hung out, smoked weed and played cards all day. I was introduced to Jen by my friend's sister. After seeing her over at their house a few times, I started to notice that she would leave to go home at a certain time. Once I picked up on her routine, I pretended to be tired coincidentally around the same time and would eventually work myself up to offer her a ride home.

I used to go home every night thinking of a way to get with Jen. Seeing her over at my friend's house made me want to be there every day just to see her. I assumed that she didn't have a boyfriend because all she ever did was hang out with my friend's sister. I just had to wait for the right time to say something to her without ruining my chances. One day, I overheard her say that she was getting ready to leave and I told her that I was also getting ready to go myself. So, I asked her if she needed a ride home. It just felt like it was the perfect opportunity to make my move. She didn't live very far from my boy Ronnie's house, but this was my chance. This was my big break to ask her out. After taking her home a few times in my white 1997 Altima I had back then, I knew that I had her. We started dating and before you knew it, we became a couple and we have been together ever since.

We've been through a lot of crazy shit together. I was still heavily involved in the drug game when we met, but that never seemed to bother Jen. In fact, I knew she was really the one for me because she never tried to change me. She accepted me for who and what I was from day one. Like my Ita, I knew she loved me unconditionally. She loved me just the way I was. It felt so good to find someone that loved me like that, unconditionally, regardless, she was my *"ride or die"* and has always been ever since, that first ride home back in 1998. She has always been right there next to me. Most women would have freaked out after bringing them around crack houses where all you would see were dealers cooking and bagging up crack or people smoking it. Jen would walk right in along with me and be like *"Hey everyone, how are y'all doing today?"* There we were at a crack spot and she was greeting everyone like we had just walked into a church. But knowing that she would ride along with me no matter what made me trust her more than anyone else in the world.

I remember I would drive through two towns just to go and pick Jen up from school only to drop her off around the corner. There were times when other students would ask her if I really drove that far just to drop her off around the corner from her school and she would always just respond with a simple, *"yes."* But I didn't care about what anyone thought. What mattered to me was that I had found the person that I wanted to be with and that's all that really mattered to me.

Jen and I have really been through a lot of crazy and tough times, but in the end, we knew that we were unbreakable. It was never about her or me, it was about us. I have and will always give Jen a lot of the credit for where I am today. Had it not been for her, I wouldn't know where I would be today. She has always been my toughest critic. But no matter what, she has been with me. She has been with me when I was broke, rich, fat, skinny, locked up and free. She always gives it to me straight. When everybody around agrees with me just to make me happy, she always keeps it real with me. Although at times we sometimes disagree in certain situations, I know that all she wants is what is best for me.

I remember one day Jen coming over to me and telling me that there was a parked car that looked very suspicious in front of our house. I was scared as fuck. I thought it was a narc car watching our house. I had a lot of drugs in the house and I was beginning to stress out. I didn't want to go back to prison. Especially now that I had her in my life. So, to calm me down, Jen walked right outside and went straight to the car to ask them to explain why they were just sitting there parked and watching our house. In my mind all I kept thinking was, damn, my girl is crazy for going to the car and talking to the narcs that way! It turned out it wasn't a narc car. It was my cousin's wife waiting for my grandmother to arrive from the airport. We couldn't stop laughing about it once we found out who it really was. I was really shook. But that was Jen. She didn't play that shit.

After Jen graduated from high school, she ended up moving in with me at my parents' house. That was around the same time that she had a lawsuit that was pending due to being bit by a neighbor's dog. When she turned eighteen, she ended up getting $36,000. Everyone around her wanted to get a piece of that money. I remember that there was a house right down the street that we were looking to purchase. I believe at that time the house was only going for $10,000. We tried asking our family members for some advice about buying a house, but it seemed like they all wanted handouts instead. Jen ended up using some of the money to get her mom an apartment. She even ended up buying her all the furniture too. Her money was all gone in less than a year. Yes! We went through all that money in less than a year.

Once the money was gone, I got right back into the streets heavy again. When Jen and I would get into arguments, she would always yell at me and tell me to go and get a real job or to go and be a cab driver like my dad. If the argument got really serious, she would just go right back to her mother's house. Lucky for me, we had Cartoon Network. Jen's favorite. Jen didn't have all the channels that I had at my house. So I always knew that it wouldn't be long before she would end up coming back once she was no longer mad at me.

One day, Jen and I along with her Mom and Stepdad were taking a ride to the store in her 1992 Toyota Corolla wagon. Out of nowhere, a car came crashing into us. We ended up having yet another lawsuit for $15,000. Jen and I got $5000 each, and the other $5000 went to Jen's parents, we had to wait almost five years to get it though. In between all of that, I ended up getting arrested again for an armed robbery charge that I didn't even have anything to do with. I was just at the wrong place at the wrong time. Thankfully, the case went all the way up to the grand jury, and the charges were finally dropped. However, soon after that, I ran into some people that were involved in doing credit card fraud. Me, being the hustler that I have always been, didn't even hesitate to dive right back in.

"Never count another man's pocket"

The Big Betrayal

I had been running the streets and selling drugs for almost ten years before I decided to switch things up. Unfortunately, I once again used my business smarts and took my talents to the streets. It was my sense of entitlement that led me to get in trouble again, but sometimes people learn the hard way. With the opportunity to make more money in a much safer way than drugs, I left the drug hustle and chose a more profitable risk with credit cards. To me, it was simple. You get a black box; you swipe a customers card and then you would just send it over to make a duplicate. There was nothing hard about it. I felt much safer with this new scheme than I ever did standing on a corner or driving around making drug sales all day.

The way that the credit card scheme worked was very simple. We would usually give the black box to someone who worked at a business where customers would be using their credit cards to pay for their purchases. Let's say for example a restaurant. The customer would hand their card to the waitress, the card would then be brought to the back and get swiped on the restaurant debit card machine and then again on the portable black box to make a duplicate. Once we printed out the duplicate, we would then use the card as if it were our own. By the time the customer realized their information had been stolen, it would be about a month later, when they got their credit card bill.

I decided to go into the credit card business full time. Once I realized that the bottom line to this was extremely lucrative, I was like credit cards is where it's at. The amount of money that I was making made drug dealing feel like a waste of time. I had a great run but it all came to halt when I put my cousin on. But this whole run was instrumental in the destiny that was set for me.

But this whole run was instrumental in the destiny that was set for me.

A cousin of mine came to me and asked me if I could put him onto making money. At that time, my cousin *Lito* and his sister had been working at a restaurant, so I figured that it would be a perfect idea to put him on to the credit card scheme that we had been running.

Lito, who I was raised with back in the Dominican Republic when I was living with my grandparents, was in a desperate situation and wanted to make some quick money. He explained to me that his sister, who was also my cousin, had gotten pregnant by this guy named Axis. He was not someone approved of by her father. To make matters even worse, his dad had also found out that Lito was gay. My uncle was a very masculine man. Once he had heard that his daughter was pregnant and that his son was gay, he decided to divorce his wife and move back to the Dominican Republic. Since he was a cousin I could trust, I put him on and he began to make a lot of money right away.

My cousin, in the first week, made close to $15,000. He was beyond excited. He was making money he had never even heard of. Once he realized how much money he was making, he came to me and said,

"Cuz, I want to take this money that I made with you and get into selling ecstasy."

That was around the time when ecstasy (also known as MDMA and Molly) started to really hit the streets hard. It quickly became very popular. I told him that I didn't want to get involved in dealing drugs anymore because I was doing really well with the credit card hustle. And besides, that's when they had turned possession of ecstasy into a federal case if you were caught dealing it. After that conversation, I went a couple of months without hearing from my cousin. He was gone. Just like that. I thought it was strange, but thought nothing of it. Boy was I wrong.

It wasn't until I ran into him again at his sister's baby shower that I was finally able to ask him where he had been the past few months. But before I spoke to him, Jen had walked over to me and asked me if I had noticed anything weird while at the baby shower. At the time, I really didn't understand why she was asking me that. Then she asks, *"Don't you think it's kind of funny that no one is taking pictures with us or even paying any attention to us?"*

Mind you, I'm the one that paid for the baby shower and we had even been there all day setting everything up, but once Jen put that thought in my head, things did feel a little awkward. It was my family though, so I never thought that there was anything crazy going on or any real reasons to be concerned.

A few minutes later, my cousin walked over to me and we began talking. He just went on and on, giving me all of his reasons for not being around the past few months and before you knew it, we moved on from the topic and just kept talking about other things. Out of nowhere, he says to me,

"Yo cuz, I need to make some money and I want to get back into the credit card business again. Can you help me out?"

Without hesitating, I told him to come by my house on Tuesday and that I would give him the black box. The baby shower was on Sunday, so two days later, he ended up coming by my house like I had asked him to.

While upstairs in my bedroom, I handed my cousin the black box and he told me that he would get back to me in a couple of days. Everything seemed ok at the time. Again, it was my cousin, there was nothing strange about it. Little did I know, Lito was wearing a wire while the secret service sat right outside my house listening to everything second of our conversation. I was totally unaware and never in a million years would I have ever thought that my little cousin would set me up.

The very next day, while I was standing across the street from my house by the Blockbuster Video store waiting for a friend to pick me up, I noticed that there was a black Corsica slowly moving towards me with two white guys in it. While driving towards me, the car ended up hitting the wall for some reason. I took off running. When I looked back, I noticed that they were now chasing me on foot. My mind was racing. I just kept running until I reached and jumped the fence in the back of my house. I was able to run in with literally enough time to slam the door right in their faces. Later on they asked me, *"How did your chubby ass beat us running?"* I told them, *"It was my Jordan's."* LOL I ran upstairs and just started to tear everything up and flush it all down the toilet.

At the house that we had been living at, there was a metal door downstairs that you had to get buzzed in from. It was a secured door. It took them about twenty-five minutes to finally make it upstairs because our landlord at the time didn't let them come in without a warrant. That had given me enough time to get rid of all the evidence. They ended up finally getting the warrant and made their way upstairs where I was at by then. I had been sitting down on my bed waiting for them to come in.

One of the agents said to me, *"You think you're slick right? Don't worry about it, we have everything on tape already."*

I asked him, *"What do you mean on tape?"*

He responded and said, *"You heard me, we have you on tape, your cousin gave you up. We got you."*

I had no idea that my cousin had been arrested for selling drugs in New York and had turned informant. I also didn't know that when it came to credit card fraud, money laundering or counterfeit bills that it's the US Secret Service that deals with those types of crimes. It was then that I began to play everything back in my thoughts and it all started to make sense. All those months that I had gone without seeing my cousin was because they had been trying to get him to snitch on other people in order for him to avoid going to prison himself.

By the time everything was over, my cousin had given up five people. My brother and I were two of the five. All I kept thinking to myself was that I had done so many things in my life. I'd sold all kinds of drugs and even had my own crack spot. I'd pretty much been dealing drugs since I was twelve years old. I had even caught an armed robbery case that I was able to beat. I mean don't get me wrong, my parents gave me a good life. There was always food on the table, we always had a roof over our heads, but my parents were blind to everything that I was into. They had no idea of anything illegal that I had been doing for so many years. My brother Luchi and I had been dealing in the streets to the point where we didn't really need to bother our parents for anything. We did the normal things like celebrate Christmas and they would give us a few dollars here and there. But never in my mind did I ever think I was going to go down like this.

"Real Estate is a numbers game."

Hotel California

It had been three long stressful years since I had been arrested for the credit card scheme. Although I was facing some serious time in a federal prison, I still had to continue to find a way to survive. Life was a little fucked up for me at the time. This situation was a lot different for me. I'd had a little experience with doing state time, but this time I was dealing with the *Feds*. I didn't know what to expect from them. They deal with things entirely different than state courts. When it comes to the *Feds,* they'll leave your ass out there stressing and probably hoping that your dumbass continues doing stupid shit so they can add more charges or gather more information.

The one thing that the *Feds* love though, is someone who is willing to become an *informant.* In fact, one of the first things the public defender said to me was that the only way to do little to no time in the federal system was to become an informant. I told him from the start that I wasn't planning to snitch on anyone. After a few meetings with him, we decided to go and hire attorneys from Paterson instead. These guys were the total opposite. They made it very clear that they didn't want to represent a snitch in court. I had never snitched before and definitely wasn't planning on it. I had always been the loyal type to everyone and anyone that I had ever come across throughout my entire street life.

The guys that I had been running with during the credit card scheme were all older and had families at home. I didn't have any children at the time myself. All I was worried about leaving behind were Jen and my parents. That's all I cared about. I was going to do my time like I always had in the past. The only thing that kept bothering me was that when I had been arrested before, it was because I got caught slipping. What made this time even worse was that it was a family member that ratted me out. It wasn't an enemy, not a stranger, or even a crack fiend. It was FAMILY, I couldn't believe it. There's nothing in this world that could be worse than that when it comes to the streets. That's what really fucked me up.

Although I had been waiting around for the day to turn myself in to the federal authorities, I was still out there running the streets continuing to make money as if I didn't already have prison time pending. I've always been the hardheaded type and making money was always my thing.

The only difference now was that I had to be a lot more careful with whom I dealt with. I knew that the *Feds* were still watching me, but what else was I supposed to do? I wasn't just going to be sitting around doing nothing all day. I had to make sure that Jen and my parents were all ok before I had to go in. It was a great risk that I was taking. But I had been taking risks my whole life. If you knew me personally, you wouldn't expect anything less from me.

After going back and forth with the court and my attorneys, they had finally come up with a date and time for me to turn myself in at the Newark Federal Court to the U.S. marshals. My attorneys were useless. They didn't help my case at all. All they did was just take my money and I still ended up doing all the time. What these idiots failed to tell me was that I could have waited another few weeks to turn myself into the facility where I was going to be doing all of my time. But at least in my thoughts I now knew when I was going in. It wasn't easy to deal with knowing that I was going to be leaving Jen and my parents to go away to prison.

On the morning of January 3, 2005, Jen and I got married at city hall in Passaic New Jersey. It was an honor to have been married by "*The Great Mayor of Passaic*" Sammy Rivera. I believe that he was and remains one the best mayors the city of Passaic has ever had. Ironically, years later just about the time I was being released from prison, he was going into prison himself, who would've known. Regardless of what he went through and people judging him for ending up in prison, in my eyes, he was always a great man because of all the things he had done for the community.

Marrying Jen should have been one of the happiest days of my life. After the wedding ceremony we went to Alexis Steakhouse in Clifton, New Jersey with our friends and family for lunch. I could barely eat the chili fries that I had ordered because it was only a matter of hours before Jen had to drive me to Newark County Jail to turn myself in. Most people probably wouldn't understand why I would have wanted to marry Jen on the same day that I had to turn myself in, but a few weeks prior to our wedding, she had told me that she was pregnant. If you asked her, she would probably tell you that I was just trying to trap her in. But I just thought it was the right thing to do. I feared that my daughter wouldn't have my last name if we would not have been married.

Jen and I left the steakhouse around 3pm. My brother Luchi was also going to be getting dropped off at the courthouse by his girlfriend. It was approximately a twenty-minute ride from the steakhouse to the jail. It was probably the worst ride I had ever taken in my life. Most married couples would be heading to their honeymoon after getting married. Here I was saying goodbye to my now pregnant wife to go into federal prison. I felt like shit having to leave her alone and pregnant when she needed me the most. But like I have always said, Jen was my *ride or die*. She had always been the strongest woman I had ever known. I gave her a kiss and hugged her tight before turning around and heading into the jail.

When I finally got in front of the judge, I really didn't have much to say. I just took full responsibility for what I had done. I took a small chance to see if the judge would have a little sympathy towards me and explained to him that I had just got married and that my wife and I were expecting our first child. He didn't care about what I had to say. His response to me was,

"That was an honorable thing to do." Yet still sent me away to prison. It was worth the shot, although I wasn't really expecting him to feel sorry for me in any way.

After being processed in Newark, I was then taken to Passaic county jail. This had to be one of the dirtiest jails to ever be locked up at. It was way overcrowded. It was dirty as hell. The toilets didn't work and there was one sink for the 120 inmates that were being held there. You could hardly breathe in that place due to the smell of shit and urine. I had heard many stories about this place prior to going there. But it was far worse than what people had said. It was just a horrible situation all the way around.

I ended up getting the top bunk of a three-man bed. I remember that it had started raining and that the roof above me had a leak. Out of all the beds in the unit, it was only leaking on top of mine. All I could think about at that point was me having to deal with that shit for two years and saying to myself continuously, *"God please help me!"* The other thing I couldn't stop thinking about was, *"Damn I should have finished those damn chili fries."*

Due to my attorneys having me turn myself in almost thirty days early, I was bounced around from facility to facility for about six weeks. Those assholes failed to get that information from the court to pass it on to me. So for that reason, I was unable to speak to my pregnant wife for about eight weeks due to the way the system works in federal penitentiaries. There was nothing that was going right for me from the start. To make matters even worse for me, the counselor at the facility was out on a two-week vacation so I couldn't even get one phone call to her.

I didn't know too much about federal prisons and how everything worked. Had I known prior that I could have just waited to self-surrender at the facility where I would be doing my time, and I wouldn't have gone through all the issues that I had been dealing with. I went from turning myself in Newark, to being transferred to Passaic County, right after that it was Trenton County Jail, and Camden County. All within a four-week period.

After going through a total of eight weeks of being transferred from jail to jail, we were finally leaving the last holding facility and heading over to FCI Philadelphia. About sixty-eight of us had been chained up and shackled from our hands to our feet and put on a bus the size of a Greyhound. I remember it being about twenty degrees outside that day and they had us out there in t-shirts. We stopped at three different facilities while dropping off inmates at each one of them. Finally, there were eight of us left on the bus. There was this guy on there with us who had been schooling us the entire time on how to make it in a federal prison.

We had started with sixty-eight inmates and now we were down to only a few of us. As we got closer to the prison gates of the facility that we were going to be dropped off at, I noticed that everyone's faces looked defeated. My brother and I were the only ones doing short time while everyone else was doing all the way up to thirty years. Right before having to get off the bus, the radio had been turned on and through the speakers I heard the song, 'Hotel California' by Eagles when we got to FCI Fairton. To this day that song still reminds me of that sad day, and everybody's faces on that bus.

'Hotel California' by Eagles when we got to FCI Fairton. To this day that song still reminds me of that sad day, and everybody's faces on that bus.

The devil wasn't done with me just yet though. Right when I thought that everything was finally getting better, it turns out that these assholes apparently had found out that there was something wrong with my paperwork. I thought they were just fucking with me and trying to make my life miserable. They told me that apparently, I still had an open case from back in 1998, that hadn't been resolved. They explained to me that no inmate could be at a federal prison camp if you still had a detainer. I ended up being thrown in *'the hole'* for two weeks, I still had not spoken to my wife.

Although I hadn't talked to Jen in six weeks, she was constantly calling the jail to make sure that I was ok. When she found out that they had thrown me in the hole for a situation that had already been resolved, she began running around, making phone calls and doing everything that she could to prove to them that I had no open case that was pending. It sucked being in prison and not being able to control anything. When you're locked up behind those walls, you belong to them. They don't care if you're sick, stressed out or dying. All you are to them is a number and another thug off the streets. My *ride or die* Jen was the only one by my side.

By the time I was able to finally get a visit from Jen, fourteen weeks had already gone by. She was about four months pregnant and her belly was already beginning to show. We were so happy to finally see each other. She didn't really appear to be stressed out like I thought she would have been. Jen has always been a strong woman. The only thing that she was really concerned about was our parents. It wasn't easy for them to deal with the fact that I was in prison.

Right before I had turned myself in, we had finally received the lawsuit money from the accident. Jen and I had agreed that we weren't going to try to buy a house until we had kids. Now that she was pregnant, we had decided that we were going to buy a house with the $10,000 that we had received and move out of my parents' house. Back then it really didn't take much to be a homeowner. Those were what I have always called *"the wild cowboy days"* of real estate. It was much easier to buy a house back in those days compared to everything that you have to go through today.

Those were the days when you could get a stated income mortgage loan based on your credit. Honestly, we really had no business buying a house at that time. There was way too much going on. The process took longer than what we thought, and it was all being done around the time when I had already turned myself in. I didn't know if I was going to be able to do the closing while I was in prison. Then, while we had been going back and forth trying to do the closing, my restitution from my case pops up. At that point, the banks shouldn't have even given me a loan without paying that off first. We didn't have the kind of money at the time to take care of that issue. I was surprised that they were even trying to do business with me while I was locked up. But for some reason, the bank didn't really care. 2005 was a wild time in real estate yet somehow, we managed to make it happen.

Jen and I had finally become homeowners. The seller of that house had been so cool with us that he even let Jen move in even before the closing was finalized. Although I was away doing my time, 2005 was a great year for us, even though I couldn't be there to celebrate like I wish I could have. Jen and I had gotten married, we were expecting our first baby and now we had our own house. I was beginning to feel like everything was coming along and getting better for us. In fact, we still have pictures of Jen fixing the floors while she was pregnant. Since I wasn't there for Jen in the house, both of our parents helped out as much as they could.

I felt really bad that Jen had to deal with so much without me being there for her. Although she never complained, I knew that none of it was all that easy for her. I can't imagine what she must have gone through having to carry a baby and do all of the things that came with fixing up the house. It stresses me out just thinking about it. To make matters worse, none of the people that I ran with in the streets bothered to come and see me, or even send me a few dollars to hold me down. All the support I got while I was away came from Jen and our parents.

I went to prison for what I believed at the time was for helping out a family member who had come to me for help, and because of it, I wasn't able to even see my daughter Taylor being born. That to me was and has always been one of my biggest regrets. I will never know what it is like to hold your baby on the day they are born. I will never know what it is like to look into my wife's eyes on the day our first child was born and tell her I love her and tell her how I am proud of her. I had kept my mouth shut and never snitched on anyone else behind the credit card scheme because I didn't want them to be away from their families and it turns out I was the one who was hurt the most. And that's when I learned the truth behind the word *loyalty*.

"Don't be a penny pincher."

Luchi

*B*eing locked up in a prison away from your family is usually considered the worst part about doing time. That's what I've always believed at least. You would think that having a really close family member doing time right there next to you would be a blessing right? I mean, what could go wrong? Most inmates were lucky if they even got to see any family members come to visit them while they were in prison. As for me, well, I had my pain in the ass brother Luchi. At that time, it was unheard of for family members to be locked up together. I knew it was going to be a shit-show right from the start.

Here I was dealing with all the shit that had been thrown my way the first two months of my *bid* and now I had to deal with my crazy brother and all of his adventures. Although my brother had been sentenced to only serve ten months, you would have thought he had been sentenced to do life in prison. Every day it was something new. If it wasn't him arguing with another inmate, he was on the phone fighting with his crazy-ass girlfriend. The worst part about it was that each and every time he got into something, I was the one that had to come and save his ass.

When we went in to do our time, he had been dating this girl for only a few months. He was *sprung* out over her. She had him by the balls. Every chance he got he was on the phone arguing with her over the dumbest things. He would call her and then be on the phone screaming at her all day while the other inmates watched and listened in only to end up making fun of him. You have to understand, prison is boring, so any chance that an inmate could use to get their attention away from having to deal with their own frustrations, trust and believe they were going to fuck with you until they couldn't laugh about it anymore.

My brother is smaller than me and one year younger, so I always ended up fighting his battles and protecting him. He was crazy over her. One day, he comes to me and says,

"Yo! Guess what, my girlfriend made me get a DNA test."

I asked him, *"How the hell can she make you go and get a DNA test when her daughter was already five years old when you guys got together?"*

He was so in love with her that he would have done anything that girl would have asked him to do. He turns to me and says,

"Well, you never know, right?"

I said *"What the fuck do you mean you never know? You didn't even know her five years ago!"*

That's how sprung he was over this girl, and after all the bullshit she made him go through, she only ended up holding him down for 3 months before she left him.

My brother is a fucking character. I remember one day the guards were doing count right before dinner. The counselor gets on the loud speaker right after the count had been completed and says,

"Oh yeah, and to that guy who asked me about getting married while he's in here, you fuckin loser, you won't be able to do that in the next couple of weeks, but I'm not gonna say your fuckin name, you fuckin loser."

Right before he finishes doing count, he follows up with,

"Yeah Luis Piña, you fuckin loser."

All that could be heard was over 120 inmates hollering and laughing at the same time.

"Everything for sale has a profit."

Brooklyn Tiger Tails

*W*hile in prison, I really spent a lot of time sitting around reminiscing about the past and sharing stories with other inmates. Aside from missing Jen and my family, I tried to find ways to stay positive and pass time. Humor does help relieve the stress while your locked up. It made things a lot easier for me knowing that everything was going well with my family back at home, so between all of that, I was just focusing on my release date and trying to figure out what I was going to do once I was free. Trust me, being incarcerated is the worst of the worst. I don't care who you are or how many times you have done time in the past. No one wants to be in prison.

I often thought back to the memory of when a bunch of us decided to experiment with PCP. They used to call it leaky leaf back then. I remember there were 8 of us packed like sardines in a white Nissan Pathfinder and listening to the Hip Hop Artist Nas. We were going about one hundred miles an hour over the George Washington bridge. This drug had me in another world and high out of my mind, I only remember counting every single light bulb that we drove past. Everything was in slow motion. We drove to 42nd Street in the city and hung out there, which was a risk in itself. This is Pre-Giulliani Era in the city where Times Square was a place that frequented the calls of drugs, hookers and anything else seedy, it was like a frisky free for all Flea Market.

As soon as we got there, the idea was to check out girls. There were strip clubs on every corner, New York City was wild at that time. We were on 42nd with a whole selection of girls in front of us, we even got a little flirty with the girls and did what guys do at a strip club, and then all of a sudden a girl comes up to us and says *"Do you guys know where you're at?"*

We all answered *"Yeah, we're on 42'nd Street."*

She says, *"No you're not, you're on 44th St and this is the Chicks with Dicks block."*

With no exaggeration, we all started throwing up. We couldn't believe that we had actually been feeling up on a bunch of transexuals.

We ended up leaving there and driving down to Hunt's Pointe, Bronx. We were all just going around in a van looking for something to get into. Now looking back, it seems like the only focus I had back then was making money, by any means necessary or chasing girls. As crazy as it sounds, I remember that in this occasion when one of us ran across a chick that would give us blow jobs, all ten of us would be standing right outside the van patiently waiting for it to be our turn. Those were the crazy teenage years where I didn't care about goals, or had any idea of what I really wanted to do with my life. All I cared about was having fun and making money.

The funniest story of them all was the day we found out for sure that our cousin Lito was gay. The cousin who gave me up to the Feds. Although we had always thought that my cousin was gay, he had not officially *'come out of the closet'* at the time. I'm not against anybody being gay, it was the circumstances surrounding my cousin and the whole *"coming out"* that made it funny. I'm not sure if he thought that he was going to be judged for it or because he was afraid of what his dad would do or say. But he was only able to hold onto that secret until we all found out by accident. It was crazy how it all went down too.

One night, while hanging out in downtown Passaic, we all decided to go and watch some of those twenty-five cent peep shows. In Passaic, NJ, porn rental shops have small booths, and back in the day you could watch porn by yourself in the store. It was sort of like a private cinema where you would walk in, and search for the type of porn you were into. Once you found the one you were interested in watching, all you had to do was put in a quarter and the video would start playing. My friend for some reason ends up watching a video where one of the guys happened to look like my cousin. A few minutes later, he comes running over to me and says,

"Shit look, your cousin is in this porn video."

I didn't believe him when he first said it. So, I put another quarter in to see for myself, and confirmed it, *"Oh shit it's really him!"*

The name of the video was "Brooklyn Tiger Tails." In the video, we saw this big black guy knocking and my cousin walking to answer the door. The man at the door says to my cousin, *"Did someone call for a plumber?"* We already knew where that story was heading. The next thing we see in the video is my cousin pulling the man's pants down and let's say the rest is a wrap. All I kept thinking to myself was, damn this is how this motherfucker is going to come out the closet! My brother Luchi, who was there with us, also ended up watching the video. We were dying laughing and kept saying in disbelief *"Lito actually does gay porn."* What was even crazier about my cousin's story was that he had used my name in the porn video. He called himself, Cesar Lito! I was like what the? You can guess!

Once all of us got a chance to watch the porn, we ended up going back home. We were so freaked out about what we had just watched. While my brother and I were in the bedroom talking about it, our mother had been listening to us through the door. Once we explained the story to our mother, she then goes and calls my aunt. Next thing you know, my entire family had heard about it in a matter of minutes. It got really crazy after that. For the next week or so, each one of them had gone down to watch the movie to verify that it was really him.

The situation was both crazy and funny at the same time. I would have never expected any of them to go down there and watch it for themselves. But I guess they really needed to see it for themselves. I thought it was hilarious sitting there and watching them trying to find the best disguises to wear so that no one would know that it was them. My brother and I telling them it was really our cousin in the video just wasn't enough.

I remember seeing my aunt and grandmother going down there wearing sunglasses and a scarf over their heads while covering their faces so that no one would recognize them. Once they all had confirmed that it was really him, my cousin had no other choice but to let the secret out about him being gay. I really found it hilarious when I had heard that Lito's mom was so embarrassed about the video that she would continue going back there to buy all of the copies that were on sell at the store, so that no one else would be able to watch them. But it didn't matter how hard she tried, the owner just kept making more copies and continued selling them.

Although my cousin probably didn't really want anyone to know at the time, he eventually ended up thanking me for making it easier for him to come out because he no longer had to live a lie anymore about being gay. Looking back at that situation, sometimes I wonder if my cousin giving me up to the feds was payback for us telling our family about him being in a gay porn. It could have been his reason, but to me it's all in the past now. The funniest part about the whole story was when my cousin's brother had actually worked himself up to go watch it for himself. He was the last one to go. He ended up running out screaming *"He was *giving that guy a blow job with my fucking shirt on that he borrowed from me!"* It was fucking hilarious.

"No such thing as a perfect deal."

What Street Code?

While doing my time at Fairton prison camp, I sometimes ran across the thoughts about how I was locked up for credit card fraud while the people we dealt with were still out there running the streets. I'm not saying that we should all have been locked up together, but what pissed me off the most was that they didn't even care to look out for me or my family while I was away. I wasn't even the top guy in this operation like the feds thought when I had been arrested.

I went in as the leader of a credit card fraud conspiracy. I kept my mouth shut and took all the weight for it. In my mind, I had done the right thing when it came to the code of the streets. As far as I was concerned, part of that code should have also been taking care of the people you ran with in the case they had been arrested or locked up in prison. These guys never took a single minute out of their day to check and see if I was ok. They didn't pay for my attorneys or ever do anything at all for me while I was in prison. I never saw or spoke to them again. That situation taught me to never trust or believe anyone when they tell you that they will always have your back. Although I was man enough to do the time for the crime that I had committed, I quickly learned that there was no such thing as loyalty when it comes to the streets.

Being away from my family made me realize that I needed to change my way of life. I had been running the streets all of my life and had nothing to show for it. I knew that I couldn't continue living my life so recklessly anymore. I was a married man with a baby on the way. I knew that I had to begin making better choices in my life compared to how I had been living my life. My situation could have always been worse than the one that I had been dealing with, but I knew that if I went back to the life of crime, I couldn't count on always getting second chances. I felt like I was very blessed to have only been sentenced to serving 18 months in prison for credit card fraud. I was also given three years probation and a $75,000 fine.

I don't believe that there is anything about doing time in prison that should make anyone proud. Not because I thought I was better than anyone else or because I was too good to be locked up. It's because it's a dead-end road, in life you don't need a prison vacation, trust me. In fact, my experience in prison was so bad that my whole view of it changed. I began to believe that going to prison was for losers. Money is obtainable, time isn't. You can never get wasted time back. I began to believe that the most important thing that we have in life is time. I didn't want to end up being one of those types of people who would be looking back into their past with regret after realizing that all they did was waste their entire lives doing nothing. The more I sat there thinking about my future, the more I began to realize that I had to start to come up with a better plan. I was about to be a father. It was for that reason that I knew I had to finally grow up and start acting like a real man.

The more I listened to the rest of the inmates complaining about the system and how they were all innocent of the crimes that they had been sentenced over, the less sorry I began to feel about myself being incarcerated. The first step that I began to take towards changing my way of thinking was to finally accept that everything that I had been through including the situation that I was in was all my fault. I could have sat around complaining about having been set up by my cousin or about my attorneys not doing enough to keep me from going to prison. My issues didn't start in 2005 when I was incarcerated. They started the moment I decided to be a look out kid for those drug dealers back when I was twelve years old.

For many inmates, prison was like going away to college. Instead of trying to better themselves and changing their way of thinking, they would sit around with other inmates who taught them how to become better criminals. Most of them would continue going in and out of prison their entire lives because they ended up going back out on the streets always thinking that they have come up with a better way to commit crimes. Now I'm not saying that all inmates are criminals. But the majority of them accept defeat. Their minds have been so conditioned, that committing crimes and making money is all they want for their life as long as they live. Although I had been one of those types of people myself, I always knew that I could do better.

Most of us used to sit around and talk about the positive changes that we were going to make once we had been released. Of course, the guards would always come around trying to kill our dreams by saying things like *"You're all criminals and will always be."* In most cases, they were right. According to the recidivism rate around that time, 5 out of every 6 inmates would end up being remanded back to prison within 9 years of being released. Although those numbers were probably real, I knew that I was not going to be part of that statistic. I would remind myself constantly that the only way felons made it back to prison was if they decided to go back to the life of crime. I didn't care about those numbers or what the guards said about us. I was done with even thinking like a criminal, the focus of real estate was a make or break decision in my life.

I was done with even thinking like a criminal, the focus of real estate was a make or break decision in my life.

After a while, I began to let go of the belief that what I was going through was all my cousin's fault. I took full responsibility. I went to prison for my own actions. I know that. I look at things in an entirely different way today than I did in the past. Yes, there was betrayal that took place that got me here, but I began thinking that everything that happens to us in life is just all part of a bigger plan. A plan like a jigsaw puzzle that needed to be pieced together in order to put my life where it needed to be. In prison I began learning more about real estate and legitimate interests so that I could provide a better life for my family. As the end of my prison sentence drew closer, I came across an inmate who inspired me to take my thoughts of real estate from dream to reality. His name is Rene Abreu.

"Struggles create greatness"

My Big Brother

*L*ooking back into my past, I began to feel like those dreams of buying a big house like the ones my dad would point at were about to become a reality. I didn't really know it at the time, but the more I talked with Rene, the more I began to understand the real estate business. Rene was a real estate mogul. He knew all the ins and outs of the business. He had never been in trouble his entire life. In exchange for some real estate advice, I gave him what I thought was good counsel in handling the life of prison. At times it takes simple street knowledge to deal with certain personalities in prison, so as Rene gave me advice, I gave him my expertise about prison life.

Rene and I connected right from the start. Although I didn't really have any experience in real estate, I truly began to feel like meeting him was not just a blessing, but that it was also destiny. He was already a millionaire by the time we met. He was what was known as a white-collar criminal, but despite his past, he was instrumental in the success that I'm living in now. He taught me everything I know today about real estate. It was a life-changing moment for me. It was then that I realized what my purpose was in life. I reflect back into my past and see how many times things could have turned out worse. For each and every crime that I had committed throughout my life, I could have easily been serving double-digit time like most of the inmates around me were.

The moment I met Rene was the moment I knew what I was going to get into once I was released from Fairton. Real estate became my passion, maybe at first it was an obsession; it completely consumed me. I had sold drugs and got caught up with credit cards because I had always been a hustler, a go getter. I had always loved making money, who doesn't? From the Polo shirts, to the flea market, to marijuana, to the credit cards. I've always been a hustler. But this time, I was going to do it legally, all legitimate. I couldn't wait to get out and get right into the business. There was nothing in my thoughts other than real estate. Everything and anything occupying my mind was now all about real estate. I felt really good about my future knowing that this time I had a real plan. But yet again, the devil was still trying to jam me up.

Right before I was supposed to get released from prison, one of the guys that I had been running with during the credit card business got caught selling fake documents. Somehow, the *Feds* tried to tie me up with those charges. They ended up pulling me out from Fairton and transferred me to MDC Brooklyn. Mind you, this was happening right before Jen was about to give birth to our daughter so all I wanted to do was go home and be there with my family. But the same way I was having issues when I had first gone in, I was now having them again when I was about to get out.

As soon as I got to *MDC*, I tried using the phone to call home. In prison, inmates have this thing where they would cut you in the line or *phone check* you while you're talking to see if you would get off the phone. If you allowed any of them to do it just once, you'll be labeled weak by everyone in the prison. I remember a gang member came from behind me and tried cutting me off in line as I was waiting to use the phone. He must have thought I was just going to let him punk me as he stood there laughing in my face. At this time, I hadn't really been in any trouble or had altercations with anyone the entire time I had been in prison. While he stood there laughing, I punched him right in his face and knocked him to the ground. He never looked my way ever again. Things just kept getting worse, when it rains it pours.

I felt like the *Feds* weren't satisfied enough with the time that I had been given. When I first got to prison, they had put me in the hole for a case that had already been resolved. And now that I was getting ready for my release, they were now pressuring me to "cop" out to new charges that I didn't have anything to do with. No matter how hard they tried, I had told them right from the start and kept my word to the very end that I was not going to plead out for anything that I had nothing to do with. After going back and forth with them, they eventually ended up dropping my case.

I felt like I was being put through hell all over again. While I was being held at MDC Brooklyn, I ended up running into this guy nicknamed *'Freddy Kreugar,'* who was a hitman for the Dominican gang *'The Wild Cowboys'*. He was a straight killer. This hitman who was actually sitting right in front of me, looked me dead in the face and said, *"You remind me of the first guy that I ever killed."*

Now I'm just sitting there freaking out. I'm saying to myself, fuck man, why did this man have to tell me that shit?

I was only held there in Brooklyn for about three months. Freddy Kruegar and I eventually got to know each other and became close friends for that little period of time. Aside from him, I also ran into other people like Steve Madden, Peter Gotti, Peter Bacanovic, and Kenneth "Supreme" McGriff just to name a few. But once the charges for the fake documents had been dropped, they ended up transferring me right back to Fairton to finish my sentence.

I couldn't wait to get back to meeting up with Rene and continue where we had left off regarding the real estate business. But as I was nearing the very end of my sentence, I had finally come across the greatest news that would make everything negative in my past just disappear from my thoughts. On July 1st, 2005, Jen gave birth to our daughter Taylor. It was the happiest moment of my life. To this day it breaks my heart that I wasn't there to hold her when she was born. Instead, I was in prison, wearing a green prison uniform the very first time that I held her in my arms. It immediately changed my life forever. Holding my sweet baby girl that day, I decided to become not just a better man, but also a better husband to my wife, and the best father a daughter could ever have.

"A life is a story lived."

The Dream

*T*hings were finally beginning to look much better for me after all that I had gone through. Although I was only in prison for a short period of time, so much had changed since the time that I had turned myself in. Jen and I had purchased our first house, our daughter Taylor was born, I no longer wanted anything to do with the street life, and of course, I was now on a mission to pursue my dreams of getting into the real estate business.

In January of 2006, I was released to a federal halfway house. I ended up being there for about sixty days before finally going home. When I first arrived at the halfway house, the first thing that they did was assign me to a counselor. Once I went through the orientation phase, the next thing they did was push me to go out and find a job. When I mentioned to my counselor that I already knew the type of work that I was going to be looking for, she said *"Don't worry about it, we already have a job for you."*

Standing there confused, I asked her, *"What do you mean you already have a job for me already?"*

She said, *"Your wife got you a job at this factory in Mahwah."*

Jen wasn't playing. She knew that I was going to be coming home to a lot more responsibilities compared to the way things were prior to me going in to do my time.

Jen always knew I hated working. I had always been into making easy money and she knew that. But she wasn't trying to hear any of that this time around. Jen had always considered me to be a dreamer, who never wanted to have a real job. She wasn't wasting any time trying to get me to work from the moment I was released. But of all things, she finds me a job doing manual labor at a warehouse. That was not in my plans. The funny thing was that on the day I was supposed to start the job, they never came to pick me up. I was happy as hell. I didn't want to work a back-breaking job anyway. I just wanted to get right into doing real estate.

On the other side of my halfway house there was another halfway house just for state inmates.

The one that I was in was only for federal inmates. After a few days of meeting with my counselor, I had explained to her that I had met this guy in prison that really inspired me, and that all I wanted to do was get into real estate. I ended up running into another counselor who was in charge of assisting inmates searching for employment. Her name was Ms. Cobb. She was really cool with me. When she had heard about my plans, she told me that there was this guy who would come around to the state side house and recruit inmates who were interested in doing mortgages. That really caught my attention.

I eventually ended up running into the man and explained my situation to him. Although I was on the federal side, he still hired me right on the spot. Aside from that job, I also ended up finding a part-time job as a stocker at Banana Republic in the Willowbrook Mall in New Jersey. When I was released from the halfway house and finally made it back home, I continued doing both jobs for a few more months. I hated the job at the mall. I hated that I had to wake up at 4am to go to work while everyone else slept peacefully. Every morning, I would get out of my bed so pissed off that I had to be up that damn early. I would walk around the house stomping and making as much noise as I could just so that everyone else had to be up too.

If I couldn't sleep, no one else was going to be able to sleep. Even the dog had to get up.

After a few months, the job dealing with mortgages had really taken off. We started making a lot of money. We had a group of inmates who had just been released and were now doing mortgages. It was crazy. They had all just come out from prison and had access to a lot of people's personal information. But the customers never had any idea who was on the other end of the phone call. We had made it seem like we were all working from a call center for a mortgage company when in fact, most of them were actually doing it right there from the halfway house.

As for me, I hit the ground running. I had a lot more experience in real estate than everyone else. I was averaging between $10,000 - $20,000 a month on commission. I really had no business handling people's personal information due to the fact I was still on probation for fraud. But I had to feed my family. I considered it a blessing to have found that job and to be making as much money as I was. The risk was worth it.

A few years later, under President George W. Bush. the market ended up collapsing and we ended up in the financial crisis. When the market hit rock bottom, the houses that were once going for $400,000 were now going for as low as $20,000. After giving it some thought, Jen and I decided to use the last of the money we had saved up to open a Cuban Restaurant. That lasted for about a year and a half. The only good thing that came from it was that I had become addicted to watching Telenovelas, which are the Spanish versions of American soap operas like *'Days of our Lives'*. Other than that, it was a horrible idea. None of us knew what the hell we were doing. The only person that had some experience was Jen's mom, but that was only as a cook.

While still working at the restaurant, we had been putting some money aside. Due to the financial crisis, the banks weren't lending out any money and everyone was running away from the real estate market. At that time, we had two houses that we could no longer afford. We weren't making enough income. We ended up losing two of our houses to foreclosure. Jen was pissed. She kept telling me to stop being

As crazy as it seemed, I saw the financial crash as the perfect opportunity to buy another house, so we ended up buying the house for $20,000.

a *dreamer* and to go be a cab driver like my father. Give up on my dream? Hell no! I didn't listen. I had been on a mission since I was released from prison and wasn't going to let anyone side track me, even if it meant not listening to my closest ally. As crazy as it seemed, I saw the financial crash as the perfect opportunity to buy another house, so we ended up buying the house for $20,000.

After just 30 days of owning the house, we ended up selling it and making a $70,000 profit. We shut down the restaurant the very next day. I did whatever it took to make that first deal happen. I sold my car, borrowed money from anyone who was willing to lend it to us, and even pawned Jen's wedding ring. *Yes, you read that correctly, I pawned her wedding ring.* We did whatever we had to do in order to make that first deal happen. That was how my first real estate deal went and the rest was history. I've been doing it ever since.

"Risks never taken are opportunities missed."

Valuable Lessons

*T*oday, we manage close to twelve hundred properties. I have been doing real estate now since 2006. When I first started, I had no credit. In fact, I rarely had any experience. I have no college degree. All I have is a high school diploma and a prison record. But I have always been a hustler at heart, and that's something that no one could ever take away from me. Regardless of my struggles in the past, I always promised myself that I would never stop trying to make a better future for myself and my family. I always saw how my parents did whatever it took, without ever complaining, to take care of us. My parents were always there for us, and that's what I wanted for my daughter. In fact, I wanted more than that.

I have a great team. I have many family members and close friends that have been there from day one to help me. That to me was always very important. Without a team that I could trust, none of this would ever be possible. I've always known what it was like to struggle. Giving other people a chance was my way of giving back. In fact, I also know what it feels like to have nothing. One of the best lessons that came from all of this was that if I ever wanted to see my community grow and be more positive, I had to go no further than to help those in my own neighborhood. Once I got myself in the position to be able to reach out and get them off the streets and onto a better path, I didn't hesitate to do so. Most people will view that as me just giving them a job. I saw it as me saving some of their lives. Paterson, New Jersey isn't the easiest place to live, never mind be successful.

It had always been easy in the beginning for Jen and me to manage everything on our own. She was all I really had. But once we began to expand, we knew that we had to reach out to our closest friends and family members to help us out. Not only was the business growing, I also felt that I was way too nice to manage all of it by myself. I have a kind heart. And as crazy and rough as this may sound, I needed a few tough people that most would consider assholes on my team to be my enforcers.

The real estate business is not always easy. Yes, you will have many tenants that are clean or are always on time paying their rent. On the flipside to that, you have the ones that you have to chase down, or the ones who will hold a gun to your head because they don't want to pay. They're just a couple of things that we have dealt with and witnessed personally. Not all of our properties that we bought were in rich and high-end neighborhoods. Most of them were in some of the poorest and most dangerous neighborhoods that most people wouldn't even think about driving through, let alone buying and establishing as rental property.

We take those risks though. I believe in rebuilding back our neighborhood. One of the hardest parts about real estate is also finding the best contractors to do the job. We've heard so many stories about contractors being paid and then taking their time to do the job. Even worse, I've heard about situations where they had been paid and just ran off with the money without even doing the job. Remember, every lesson is key in this business. The same things that occurred to other property owners could also happen to me. I learned from everyone else's mistakes, so I could do things a little differently. People just weren't going to respect me automatically because of who I was. Business is always business, whether it was the right or wrong

I learned from everyone else's mistakes, so I could do things a little differently.

way to do it. I take everything that comes with my business personally. If I didn't, then what would be the point in running a business?

When I find someone who is good at what they do, I try to keep them on board for all our projects. I'm not like other property owners. I don't pay half up front and then give them the rest when they are done. I like to pay them in increments. In other words, I pay them as they go. I will go and inspect what they have done, and they get paid for the work that they have completed. But before I get into the business side of things, let me explain where my dreams of getting into real estate really began. Because it wasn't like I just woke up one day and said to myself, I want to be a businessman. Most kids dream of being a doctor, a police officer, a fireman. I did too at times. I was no different in that respect.

I'll always remember the day I stood in our living room listening to the conversation between my father and the landlord that decided to sell our house back when I was a teenager. That lesson became the foundation to everything I deal with today in real estate. Although it was a situation that I would never want any other child to ever have to deal with, I also understood that it was all business and not personal. It's a crazy memory that has always stuck with me. I knew that I had come across a special lesson that would change my life forever. I really didn't know at the time, but that memory created a spark in me that has never left.

I never wanted my parents to ever be in that situation again. In fact, I wanted to help as many people in my community as much as possible, so that they would never have to struggle as much as we have in our own past. I try to always do my best to hire within my own community, so that we can build a more positive environment. Most people that come from where I came from rarely ever get a second change in life. But I also know that all people need sometimes, is the right opportunity to become better people. I feel like I am able to help change their way of life. It makes me so proud to see that they too want to see our neighborhood changed for the better also.

I know how hard it is to grow up in a tough neighborhood. I have a turbulent past myself. I know how easy it is to get stuck. We all have our own issues, but we are the only ones who can change our environment. Sitting around waiting for politicians and local authorities hasn't worked and probably never will. So, when I reach out to an individual and give them the opportunity that they may not get anywhere else, it not only makes me happy, but I also feel like I may have been able to help out an entire family from going through the situations that most of us have struggled with in our own past.

Outsiders never really understand the problems and the tough issues that we face on a daily basis. Most of them are too scared and others choose not to even care. I get it, they don't understand any of it because they don't have to deal with any of it in their own neighborhoods. But we deal with it every day. In fact, there have been many times throughout my life that those situations ended up on my own doorsteps. I too have had many close calls. For some reason, I was blessed enough to make it out, so that I could become the person I am today.

For me to sit back and watch my city die while some kill each other and others desperately struggle, while I have the opportunity to save them is not an option for me. I love giving people the opportunity to live happier lives. Don't get me wrong, we also run across people who are accustomed to their negative ways and hate to see me coming around trying to clean up the neighborhoods where they have been comfortably selling drugs and committing crimes all their lives. But that doesn't stop me from still going in and buying houses in those types of neighborhoods.

Through it all though, I have been able to get many people to change and help us out with making their community better and safer for everyone. Even some of my own family members who have a criminal history needed the opportunity. It was always a win-win situation for all of us. Although to the outsiders it may seem that we as minorities enjoy living in negative environments selling drugs, killing each other or ending up in prisons, it's really not the case. Most of the people I grew up with were barely ever given a chance, or any other options to better their lives once they became part of the system. Most of them lived and died while struggling to survive. I saw it with my own eyes every day. So of course, nothing makes me feel better than being creative in finding positive ways for everyone to live.

I have been blessed to have the right people around me that I can trust to run my business as well. In fact, one of the best things that ever came from all of this was that I was able to buy my parents their own house. I never wanted them to have to worry about paying rent or struggle with landlords ever again. I try to do all that I can for my family. In fact, mostly everything I do, I try to keep it as close to me and my city as possible. I try to hire as many people as I can from my own community in Patterson, NJ. Nothing makes me feel prouder than making my city beautiful. It's a feeling that motivates me every day.

I could have just continued being one of those types of people who gets released from prison then goes right back to terrorizing their own neighborhood. But I'm tired of hearing gunshots. I'm tired of hearing about people I know struggling when I could have probably saved them by giving them an opportunity to live a positive life. I know that trying to change people isn't easy, but now that I'm in a position to help make a difference, I always do the best that I can. It's a struggle that I'm willing to take.

I'm a simple type of person. I hate problems. I hate to see people struggle. I'm not flashy or the type of person to look down on others just because of my success. I know what it's like to have nothing. I know what it's like to not know where you're going to get your next meal. But again, I have a big heart. If there is anything that I can do to help people out, I will. That's what motivates me to do better. Of course, none of this would ever be possible without my beautiful wife Jen, my hardworking brother Luchi and all of the other dedicated workers that we have on our team. It's not only my job keep everything in order, but to make sure that everyone does their part in a respectful and positive way, and sometimes, that can be the hardest part. Between the tenants not paying rent on time, or not paying at all, and my employees complaining about some of the situations they face daily, it makes this job a little difficult and sometimes risky to the point where things can get a little out of control.

Throughout time, I have been able to figure out most of the ins and outs of real estate. At this point at where I am today, I buy properties, and don't even go to the closing. It's pointless to me. I know that for any property that we purchase that I am going to end up having to fix or replace something in it, and that's not always the issue. I remember going to a property one day and literally tripping over a body. He wasn't dead, thank God. But the thought of having to trip over a person's body gave me an idea that I was probably going to come across many of those types of situations when it came to this business. Funny thing about that situation, was that after tripping over him, I asked him why he was there, but he was more concerned with why I was there, so I ended up having to explain to him that we had bought the house and were coming there to renovate. Turns out that he had been using the house as a place to get high. Like many drug addicts in the neighborhood did.

I try to keep everything as simple as possible for my workers. All of my units are constructed the same way. Everything that I use is the same all the way around. The cabinets are the same, the paint is the same, the carpets are the same, everything is the same. But as time goes on, I just become more and more creative. I went from buying homes to wanting to learn more about development. My first big project was when we purchased a lot where we ended up building thirty apartments from scratch. I've also partnered up with Superstar Reggaeton artist Nicky Jam and purchased another school where we are currently putting in eighty units. I can definitely say that I've come a long way. It's my passion. I'm a workaholic. I love what I do. I walk through most of my properties on a daily basis. I love to see change. I will never forget where I came from, and every and any chance that I get to put a smile on someone's face, or take away the pain that I once felt, from other people, I seize the moment, because it always reminds me of what my life could have been.

I know that many people think that part of real estate is a scam or that in due time, the truth behind it all will eventually come out where people could possibly end up doing prison time. But like anything else, if you do things the right way, you will never have anything to worry about. I don't let those things bother me. You see it on the news all the time where people are committing some type of fraud or raising the value of properties to the point where it becomes a negative situation. But that's not what we do. Everything that we do is not only one hundred percent legit, we also do our best to look out for the tenants throughout our community. We also always make sure that everyone on our team is doing the same.

I have always believed in following my dream. Everyone always talks about money. When I first started, I didn't have any money. I've had my own struggles too, but I have always understood that if you wanted a better life for yourself and for your family, that one way or another you're going to have to make it happen, like I did. Rather than relying on selling drugs or dealing with people who could have landed me back in prison, I became very careful in choosing the people that I associated with. I started from nothing too. Today, the business is worth over eighty million dollars in real estate properties. And although I have made it this far, I still want to go further. My dream is to continue moving on up and at the same time help those who want to pursue their dreams in real estate as well.

"Chase your dreams through sleepless nights."

Natural Born Hustler

I graduated high school back in 1997. Again, all I have is a high school diploma. That's it. All of my friends chose college. I chose the street life. People used to always tell me that I was choosing the wrong path. I never listened. I didn't care to listen. I've done prison time, but I have learned from my past mistakes. My story is crazy. My wife and I have been together now for over twenty-two years. She is and will always be a big part of the reason why I am where I am today. She was my *ride or die* back then and she always will be. Most people have a hard time being married to a person that they also have to do business together with, but she's a hustler just like me. In fact, when I find myself struggling with certain situations, she's the one to whom I turn. It doesn't matter what the situation is, she always finds a way to fix the problem.

I still look back to the day when Jen and I got married. It sucked that there was going to be a negative ending to our day, but going to prison was the best thing that could've happened to me. I was able to turn a negative situation into a positive one. I was there for a little less than two years. Doing the time wasn't the hard part. Being away from my family was. Like anyone that has to do time in prison, I hated that I had to be away from them. A lot of things happen when you go away, even if it's just for a short time. There wasn't a day that I didn't pray or think about my family. Thankfully, nothing really serious happened to them that would have made my time harder to serve. It was all just part of my purpose and God's plan.

I can't thank Rene Abreu enough for teaching me about real estate. He really taught me all I needed to know. I felt like it was all meant to be. He made my time a lot easier for me to deal with by taking my mind away from all the negativity that we were constantly surrounded by in prison. That time became my own college experience in a way. It's crazy how God works sometimes. Here I was in the worst place that anyone could ever be, yet I ran into someone who would change my life forever. That's usually not the case when it comes to prison. Most people come across others who plan to do the same exact things that got them there in the first place. Unfortunately, some of them won't ever make it out.

When I had been released to the halfway house back in 2005, I saw that most of the inmates that made it there would just end up being remanded back to custody because they wouldn't apply by the rules. It was easy to get caught up. Some would go out and get high or never even bother to report back. Everyday somebody new was getting *packed up*. They got a little taste of freedom and always ended up screwing it up for themselves. I had a family at home. There was no way that I was going to end up right back in the feds. My mind was set on starting a business. Regardless of how tough it was being in prison away from my family, it just seemed that everything was always working out in my favor. I mean, what are the chances that I would run into a real estate mogul and then run into a man who was recruiting inmates to do mortgages? The stars were all lined up perfectly for me. My only job was to pursue my dreams.

I was released from doing a prison bid with no money in my pocket to making $15,000 – $20,000 within a month of doing mortgages. I still remember my first loan as if it were yesterday. It was crazy. There was this little old lady who was about eighty-five years old. She was on social security at the time. As we all know, it's hard to get a loan while on social security. Somehow, I still managed to get her a loan for $400,000. Soon after that, the market went down. I found myself back in a struggle that I didn't want to face ever again. So, I did what I thought was the best thing that I could do for the moment, I went into hustling mode like I always did when I found myself in a negative situation.

Right after my first real estate deal, I went from having just one house to having about nine hundred units in what felt like a blink of an eye. Remember, I told you I am a natural born hustler. Nothing was going to get in my way. Anytime a positive thought entered my head, I would pursue it. You only live once. Me, I go hard on everything. I know where I came from and I will never forget it. I made a promise to myself that I would never go backwards in life. I began feeling more and more blessed as I got deeper into real estate. Every chance that I get to invest in it, I jump right in.

I'm not about excuses or wishing for things to just fall in my lap. I went away for less than two years and met my buddy in prison who showed me the ropes and went all out. I didn't care about how much I had to put into my business. If I saw that I had an opportunity to grow, I ran after it. I went and bought properties when the market was down, or when most of them had been destroyed and had everything stolen from them all the way down to the plumbing.

I ended up meeting this guy named Sal who's a hard money lender. He explained to me that I was doing my business all wrong by using my own money to fix all the properties. My attitude was, I had my own money and didn't feel the need to borrow or ask anyone for any favors. When I first started, I just wanted to make $5000 net a month. After two years, I went from buying one to two properties to buying five. After three years, I went from buying five, to buying ten properties. Then it went from ten to twenty and jumped all the way to fifty. I went from hitting my goal of $5000 to making $10,000 a month, to $50,000, $100,000, $200,000 and so on. I was tapped in. I started *"flipping"* houses left and right. After the fourth year, I bought my first commercial property which had twelve units, two storefronts and twenty apartments. It was a great deal. The market was still down at the time. I purchased a million plus dollar property for $400,000. It was a steal. It didn't even need much work.

Rental properties were one thing, commercial properties were an entirely different animal. Everything was based on the income of the property and not on comparable sales like residential properties. Although I bought the property for $400,000, it was actually worth $1,200,000. So, I was able to refinance and take out money in order to do what I had been doing with smaller properties, but on a bigger scale. After seeing how much I was making from commercial properties, I began buying more of them. Now that I was really into buying commercial properties, I still continued buying smaller residential properties. I just kept purchasing more and more properties until I got into developing different projects.

On a property, I like to make anything between $1500 - $2000 a month net after paying all my expenses on the smaller ones. The most important and genius idea that works for us is that I used the same styles in all of my properties. It just makes everything easy. Everyone knows what to do without me having to be leaning over their shoulders explaining it to them. All the employees on our team are very well trained. They all know everything from the layout all the way down to materials that they need. It just makes everything a hundred times easier for our business.

Not only am I getting all the materials from the same people, all of my workers can work in peace without us having to hassle them. Another one of my biggest *go to* strategies is buying some of the worst properties in the neighborhood. The worse they were, the more I wanted to invest in them. I say that because that's where I can add value, and the worse the house is, the less money

I am going to pay. Most people would just walk past these properties thinking that they would have to put too much work into them. I see them as a project. Once people saw the before and after, they were amazed by it, and that also always makes me feel good too.

When it comes to banks and foreclosures, they don't really know what the real cost of a property is. They'll look at a property and think that the house is messed up, or that it needs a lot of work, and price it based on looks. So, it was always to our advantage to go after those types of properties. It always reminded me of when I was a kid and watching other kids throwing something away because they no longer thought it was useful. We would go get it, shine it up and fix whatever it needed, and all of a sudden, they wanted it back. They no longer saw the value in it, just like the banks. I understood that the banks just wanted it off of their hands and sold. I always saw the bigger picture. That's why I love foreclosed properties. While everyone overlooked them, I invested in them and added more value to them. They say that it's always easy to get into something, but hard to get out of it. As for me, *I wanted in for the long run.*

By the time my mentor Rene Abreu ended up being released from prison in 2013, I had done millions of dollars in real estate business. When he came home, he helped me take it to the next level and buy bigger properties. We still stay in contact and he's always there for me anytime I have any questions or need help regarding the business.

"Never be afraid...Ever."

The Hood! A Great Investment

*T*he more my business grew, the better my team got. I have always kept that promise to myself. I always said that no matter how big I got or how much money I made that it was my job to make sure that I would bless others the same way that I was blessed. Most people make it big and never look back. Not me. Regardless of how well I did, I always wanted to look out for others because I know how hard it is to make it in this world. My parents raised me to believe in that. Because at any time, everything that you work so hard to build one minute could easily be destroyed and come to an end. I have learned that networking and having the right people on your side can and will always help your business grow.

I never imagined or even pictured my life getting to a point where thousands of people would know of me and respect my name. They know my name! In fact, although I had a vision and pursued it, I never imagined it to grow in the way that it has. But I also know that this is business and that it's not all about me. I always wake up every day thanking

God for putting me on this path, I also praise him for keeping me free and alive after all the things that I have been through in my past.

We never limited ourselves to just buying houses in great neighborhoods because we also try to fix up our own neighborhoods. You know, *"where our own kind of people stay"* Most of us grew up watching the rich people come in and rebuilding our rundown hoods, but then raise the prices on mortgages, so they could only rent them out to wealthy people, while *'the rest of us'* stayed trapped struggling, living in bad conditions for most of our lives. They didn't care about us. All that mattered to them was the rent money.

One day, Envy and I decided that we were going to have a ride-along. We took six buses with forty people on them per bus. As we got closer to our destination you could see the difference in their reactions. Most of those on the ride-along were shocked and couldn't believe where we were taking them. The areas that we drove through were areas where you would see drug dealers, crack heads, low-income people to no income people. You know, the type of places that you always saw on the news. Most of them quickly began asking, why they were there, in the run-down areas that seem to have no hope in getting better. I had to explain to them that this was where the real money was at. I told them that when you look at Harlem, Jersey City, Brooklyn, Southside Jamaica in Queens or even parts of Detroit, what usually happens is, investors come in and they buy up the entire block, push everyone out and fix up the neighborhood. After they are done, when you try to come back, because they have raised the prices in rent so high you could never afford it.

That's why we always encourage our people to never be afraid. Never become so afraid of buying, fixing and turning a bad neighborhood into a better place because you'll always get your money back, plus a lot more. You have to fix up and hold onto your own communities. I remember taking a lot of people on the bus ride to see an area in Atlantic City one weekend. It was crazy. Shit was so crazy and so fucked up there, we even saw this dude standing right in the middle of the street holding onto a crutch and swinging it around a chain yelling *"This is my block! I'm not getting rid of my block."* I mean, I understood where he was coming from because that's where he made his living. Even though he considered it his own, I know for sure that the people around there wanted him and anyone else out who was committing crimes or dealing drugs. Sometimes, those are some of the tough situations that we have to face. Now for him being an asshole, I bought the block and now he pays me rent. LOL.

You have to start with one house in the neighborhood. Once a neighbor sees that the house that was once run down is now looking brand new, they're going to want to make theirs better too. It sort of begins the domino effect for us once we start buying and fixing up all the houses on their street. See, most homeowners just want to collect rent. Most of them don't really understand that if they put the work in and invest in other homes in their neighborhood that eventually, everyone on that block is going to want to see the entire neighborhood looking good.

It's a lot easier said than done, but you have to start with that one house and work your way up and down until you see the progress. You have to always see the bigger picture. Eventually, once the neighborhood looks great, people like the dude swinging the chain around will find somewhere else to go and terrorize. Again, the trick to the game is to hire people within the same community that you are trying to fix up and, in most cases, it also helps keep the peace because it makes them feel better about themselves and the neighborhoods where they live.

When I first became a property manager, one of the first things I did was hire my brother to assist me. Like myself, he had no experience at all. He didn't go to school to learn how to become a property manager, but I still gave him a shot. Like I said before I'm way too nice. Whenever a tenant came to me complaining about anything, I always felt the need to help them. My brother on the other hand, well, he's the "*asshole*" and the "*harasser*". He will harass you so much that you're gonna want to pay him. He's the perfect person to have on my team because I know that we will never have an issue with collecting money when it is owed. We're both hustlers, he's just a little more aggressive than I am. In the beginning, when I had two or three properties, it was easy for me to handle and take care of the business. Once we grew, I saw a perfect opportunity to put him on because I needed a little muscle behind me. But he is also my brother, we are very close, and I knew that we could always help each other out and make the business better by keeping mostly everything in the family.

My brother oversees about 1,200 hundred properties. He's great at what he does. He's a natural. If you ask him, he'll tell you that he was born to be a property manager. When asked how he learned to become one, he says *"Well, it's like asking a drug dealer how or why they became a drug dealer. It's just another hustle."* He's been working as a property manager for so long that he's become a pro at it. He, and other family members that he has working under him have a great system where they keep track of all tenants and payments.

When he first started, he learned that social media was a great source to not only get his name out there, but to also use it for business purposes. He began promoting our business on Instagram and slowly started getting more and more tenants to fill up the vacant apartments on our properties. Being that he was once involved in the streets himself, he doesn't discriminate against anyone with a criminal record or credit history. He basically just looks at paystubs and makes sure that the tenants can afford housing and gives them a chance. He may be an asshole sometimes, but he also understands the struggle. I wasn't really into social media myself, but I do see how it helps

My wife actually created @flipping_nj for me on Instagram and it has helped our business grow much faster.

promote the business. My wife actually created @flipping_nj for me on Instagram and it has helped our business grow much faster.

We try to be as lenient as we possibly can with our tenants. Of course, there's always going to be a great chance that we're going to come across some who are going to be problematic. We do try to work with them before going to the extreme of getting them evicted. We always attempt to be as helpful as we can with them, but we also have a job to do and bills to pay ourselves. If they were ever backed up on their payments for whatever reason, it can become a problem for us as well. Not only does it make things a little uncomfortable and complicated between us, but we also have other employees that we have to pay. They always want us to understand them, but how comfortable would it be for us to tell our employees that they can't get paid because people haven't paid their rent? It's sad and it sucks sometimes, but again, business is business and they all know that the rent has to be paid regardless of any circumstances.

Collecting rent isn't always easy. Sometimes collecting rent reminds me of the street game. People act like you're just coming to their door to rob them and steal their money. I laugh at some of the excuses some of them come up with, but other times, they don't even have one. They just curse you out without even opening their door. My brother had a gun pulled on him one day while trying to collect rent from a lady out in Newark. I laugh because he said that it almost made him quit. Although it was a serious situation and it could have turned out to be worse, we still laugh about it to this day.

I can go on and on about all the crazy things that occur when it comes to collecting rent, but the tenants also try to outsmart you when you knock on their door to make them pay. All of a sudden this doesn't work or that doesn't work in the apartment, but never once did they complain about it prior to owing. I can write an entire book about all the excuses that I have heard throughout all these years in this business. Trust me, just when you thought you had heard the most creative one, there was always another one that made the last one believable. Yeah, there's a lot more bullshit that comes with it too. It's all part of the business. We knew that going into it. And most of them think that the law is on their side when it comes to trying to evict them, but we have dealt with the situation for so long, that all we have to do is contact our lawyers and quickly settle the situation in court.

I know it's hard sometimes. People just don't like paying for anything. We are also human. We also have a heart regardless of how much we try to just do our jobs. We always do our best to work with all the tenants. For example, if a tenant's rent is a $1000 and they only have $800, we try to be understanding. But like I said, at the end of the day, it's a business. We have our own responsibilities to handle too. The toughest part of this business has and will probably always be evicting people, but we have to be firm. Can you imagine what it would be like if the word got around that one tenant got away with not paying, or people heard that we let one single person get away with anything period? Picture what the rest of them will probably try to do.

People think that getting evicted is wrong. But, take a moment to look at it from our point of view. If they don't pay, we have to come out of our own pockets to pay the mortgage ourselves regardless if they pay or not. And even when we have to evict them, we still have to pay court fees, and for the eviction process. That's why prior to ever approving anyone for any of our properties, we get a copy of their license, a paystub, or even their social security check because you just never know what the future may hold. One day, they may just decide that they no longer want to pay their rent and we may have to end up evicting. But at least we have all the information that we need to make sure that we end up getting paid for what they owe us, whether it's by taking them to court or having a collection company that buys that debt and tracks them down until they eventually pay up.

It's a great business. I love what I do. In fact, we all love what we do. Sometimes it gets a little risky, but it's all part of the game. I know what we are dealing with. We may never know what we are getting into or going up against sometimes, but I believe that regardless of the situation, we will always try our best to find the best solutions. We want to be happy and have fun doing what we do. We also want to make sure that all of our tenants do too. But at the end of the day, they know rent is due at the beginning of the month, because our workers also have a family to take care of and support back at their homes.

"Always be open to learning new things."

No Day 1's

*F*rom the very beginning, my first partner in the business has always been my wife Jen. We have a very unique story that goes all the way back to when we were teenagers running the streets without any goals in life. Although the real estate dream was mine, she has always been supportive. Aside from always calling me a dreamer every time she got pissed off at me when things didn't go our way. Once she noticed that the real estate business was going well, she would no longer yell at me to go and get a job as a taxi driver anymore.

When I was locked up in prison, not a single person outside of my family ever came to see me or sent me a single dollar. When I came home from doing my time, I was all about family. I don't have any *"day 1"* friends in my life today. In fact, the only small group of friends that I have today are those that I had met while in prison and stayed in contact with. Other than that, I don't have any type of contact with anyone that I ran the streets with before 2004.

Jen has really been the only one who has stuck with me through thick and thin...*literally*. She has been with me through all of my phases in life. She stuck by me when I was dealing drugs, locked up in prison, broke, skinny, fat, and now rich. Although she can be a little harsh on me, she always gives it to me straight. She hates it when others come around and agree with me about everything. Jen always has a different perspective about everything. So anytime I come to her with an idea or a plan, she always gives me the B side.

Oftentimes I look back and reminisce about everything that we had gone through as a couple. I sometimes go back and look at the pictures that we have from when Jen was pregnant with our daughter Taylor, and doing everything that she could to fix up the first house that we had purchased. We had bought the house for cheap. We bought it from a guy who was going to lose it to bankruptcy. When we moved in, we did the basic things to make it look better. We painted and did minimal cosmetics to our floor, but the upstairs was really messed up. It needed a lot more work. It wasn't even rentable. Jen, her mom and anyone that could help her at the time began doing all the repairs that it needed to make it look good. We were just trying to get by. We weren't thinking of it as making it a career or a business. All we were thinking about was paying the mortgage, so we did everything that we could to get that second floor ready enough to be rented out. We've come a long way since.

That was around the time that I ran into Rene Abreu in federal prison. It was pretty easy back then. All people really needed to show was that they had good credit. It was the *"wild-wildwest"* era of real estate. I still remember telling Jen all about the plans that I had once I was released from prison. She believed in me, but I also knew that there was a part of her that was also a little hesitant about my ideas of going into the real estate business. I didn't blame her either. But the one thing that she never did was try to change my mind or force me to give up on my dreams.

Everything was and has always been in Jen's name. I do all the wheeling and dealing. But when it comes to signing and getting everything on paper, Jen has always handled that part of the business. She is a real business woman. She owns her own salon, and knows just as much about real estate as I do. Even though she runs around taking care of her own business, she also comes home and deals with our real estate situations too. She loves it just as much as I do. Especially when it comes to fixing up the apartments and houses. It goes hand in hand. I buy the worst properties and she enjoys making them look good.

We love this business. There is no greater feeling than when we fix up a property and get that end result. My biggest high is getting the deal done. I love that part. I never want it to stop. Jen is a big influence in the business. She has a lot of great ideas. When things don't get done in the time that she expects them to get done, she always reminds me of my short-comings. Like I've said before, she's a hustler just like I am. She loves helping others as well. She loves teaching people about the real estate game. Especially when it comes to women. She's noticed that when it comes to our seminars that it's mostly women that show up. Every chance she gets, she inspires a lot of them to get into the real estate business. She takes the business a little more personally than I do. She loves to see people win because it reminds her of when she first got into it herself.

People in this business can also be super shady sometimes, especially the realtors. For example, there was this lady in Jen's make-up class who was trying to buy a condo. Jen tried to talk her out of it because she didn't think it was a great idea for her to do. She was putting a significant amount of money down so they were making sure that she was granted the loan. They were doing everything in their power to make sure that everything went through. We knew that it was shady business. We knew that she was getting ripped off. But sometimes you have to let people make their own mistakes so they can learn their lesson.

This is the main reason why we have our seminars. We want to teach people the ins and outs of the business. We want to see everyone be happy, especially when they are spending a lot of their hard-earned money. We hate to see anyone lose. We were there at one point. We too have had our losses. And with our losses, we just want to teach people how to go about things not just the right way, but also the smarter way as well.

Before we hired my brother to go around collecting rent, it was tough. My wife and I are both softies. For example, the tenants that we had living upstairs on the second floor were sisters and I was collecting rent from each one of them separately. I thought to myself, why would we ever feel the need to do that when it was one apartment? I always had to chase down one sister for her part of the rent and then go on a wild goose chase to try to get the rest from the other one.

It was definitely a learning experience. It was really our fault though. We should have told them right from the start that since they both lived in the apartment together that they should be paying it all in full. But those are some of the little things that we both have learned. We have seen and been through almost every situation that you can come up with when it comes to tenants paying their rent. In the fifteen years that I have been in the real estate business, the worst tenants to have to deal with are women that are roommates. It has always been a problem. Jen laughs about it, but she knows how I feel.

Women who live together just never seem to get along. They always fight each other, then their problems become our problems and before you know it everything just turns out for the worst. I remember one time I went to collect rent from these two girls, they were roommates. It was on Mother's Day. They had been arguing and fighting with each other right in front of the house. I remember one of their kids went up to them and was asking for some ice cream and she says to him, *"What the fuck do you mean can you have some ice cream? I just gave this motherfucker all my money."* And I'm just standing there like, should I just go and buy the kid ice cream myself? Then the other girl comes out and she asked the lady that was standing there with the kid to borrow some money and she repeats it again, *"What the fuck do you mean can you borrow some money? I just gave this nigga all of my money."* I was standing there speechless. They used to fight all the time I went there to collect their rent. It was ridiculous.

There was this other time when this lady called me and said, *"Your brother Luchi is such an animal, he's such an asshole, I don't like the way he talks to me."* I said to her, *"I'm going to do you the favor and from now on, I will come by to collect the rent so that you don't have to deal with him personally."* Next thing you know, I had to call her and try to track her down to pay her rent. Every time I caught up to her it was excuse after excuse. One day it was someone in her family passing away or she was at the hospital. She came up with everything except the rent. Man, I couldn't believe it. She was a horrible tenant. Here I am thinking that it was my brother being an asshole so I tried to go out of my way and be Mr. Nice Guy to help her out and it turns out my brother was right the entire time. It was horrible.

Looking back, Jen was always supportive of my decision when I went into the real estate business. But there were those times when I would also get my ass chewed out when things didn't go the right way. I remember it all like it was yesterday. We had bills to pay. So, when the mortgage situations weren't paying out, I would do everything that I had to do to make things happen. Now that I have made it to where I am today in real estate, I told her that for our anniversary I wanted her to get the word *dreamer* tattooed on her ass. But she never kept her word. Now it's just a running joke between us.

"If you dream big, you'll win big."

So You're a Felon

*E*veryone says that America is the land of opportunity, but as far as it being the land of second chances, I don't believe that to be true. Because no matter how successful you are in life or and how much you give back, there are still going to be those who are still going to consider you a criminal. In the eyes of the world, my federal number is forever. And even though I haven't been in any type of trouble since my release back in 2005, there are still certain people out there who really don't believe that someone who has done prison time can change.

One day, Jen, and I had brought Taylor along with us to the bank to do a closing on a house. We already had a commitment for the loan. We were all in a room along with the bankers. Everything was going well until one of them decided that it was a great idea to bring up my past. He asked me, *"Are you done with all your jail stuff?"* Now mind you at that time, I had already been home for nearly ten years already. To make matters even worse, my name wasn't even on the loan that we had been doing the closing on. It had nothing at all to do with me.

My wife ended up grabbing my daughter by the hand and walked out of the room. My wife and I were pissed. I'm not sure if he was being serious or just trying to be an asshole and embarrass me. As soon as my daughter and wife had made it out of the room, I immediately turned to the banker and said to him, *"Bro, my daughter has no idea that I had been in prison and besides, you shouldn't even be asking me any questions because my name isn't on the loan."*

Those are the types of situations that we as former felons will have to sometimes deal with. Especially in the line of work that I'm in. You're always going to have people try to redline you and it sucks. In the beginning when I first got into the business, I would get a little upset when my past had been brought up. But to be honest, it doesn't really affect me today. My whole story is already out there, and most people pretty much know it and respect it.

To be honest though, I don't really pay attention to anything negative that anyone has to say about my past. What I don't get is why people bring it up in the first place. Had it not been for me going to prison I wouldn't have made it to where I am today. But like they say, people always wish you well, but never want to see you doing better than them. And even though some people will always view me as a felon, I don't let it stop me from helping those who have also been to prison in their past. I help them in any way that I can including trying to get them to learn about the real estate business.

Funny thing is, it's not just felons that I help or deal with. I've even dealt business with former police officers as well. One of them being this officer that I had a run in back in the summer of 1998. It was actually my first ever dealing with police brutality. I had gotten into a fight with this guy from the neighborhood after he had sucker punched me. After beating his ass, he ran into one of my friend's houses and called the police on me. When the cops arrived, there was this one overweight officer who came and threw my brother Luchi on the ground and began strangling him for no reason. I started yelling at the officer and told him to let go of my brother. The cop looked right at me and said *"Shut up you fucking spic."* He came towards me and smacked me so hard that I ended up with a black eye. I was so pissed but there was nothing that I could do.

A few weeks later, while walking around the mall with friends, I ended up seeing the officer there. This officer was actually pretty big so I knew that I couldn't beat him up by myself, so we planned to jump him once he made it to the parking lot. Somehow, we ended up losing sight of him outside. Looking back now, I thank God that we didn't find him because the last thing I needed was to be arrested for assaulting a police officer. Years later, that same officer became an attorney who I have hired to represent us on a couple of real estate deals. But it's all in the past.

I do a lot of things behind the scenes that people never really hear about. I don't walk around thinking that I am better than anyone just because I have money or because I'm known by many. In fact, one of my goals is to go to different prisons across the country as a motivational speaker to help inmates make better choices in their lives. I want to show them that I too was locked up but managed to change my way of thinking in order to make it out in the real world.

Public speaking was something that I never thought I would ever do, never mind get used to. I was a big guy and wasn't really comfortable in my own skin. I still remember the first time I ever had to do it. At first, I was very uncomfortable. It was at one of our real estate seminars and there were about 500 people in the crowd. I didn't even think that many people would come. As soon as the microphone was handed to me, my throat just dried up and my mind just went blank. Somehow, I was able to finish my speech that day. Today, I feel like I'm a pro at public speaking. I'm a lot more comfortable with it. After the first year alone, we had about 30,000 people come to our seminars. The one seminar that I remember the most was on December 15, 2019. Not only did 4000 people attend, it was also my grandfather Ito's birthday.

Before the seminars, I didn't really think nationally. I always wanted to stay as close to home as possible. After going around the country a few times and realizing that there's a lot more opportunities out there, I knew that I couldn't just limit myself to staying local. Because in order to be successful in real estate you have to be a dreamer and have a big imagination. I love going into run down neighborhoods in urban areas around the country and picturing them with beautifully renovated properties that somebody will be glad to call their home one day.

One of the most important rules in real estate is to buy under market value. I don't pay retail value for any real estate even when it comes to my personal properties. At this point I don't like paying retail for anything. The second most important rule for me in real estate is learning how to leverage your money. I didn't learn that until my second year in the business. You always want to be able to stretch your money in order to buy more with less. Real estate is the only investment vehicle that allows you to achieve that. We now own property in Atlanta, Chicago, Miami, and all over New Jersey. Those are my main markets.

In the beginning of my real estate journey, I used to let my pride get in the way of doing business. I would always get offended if a real estate agent wouldn't call me first about a deal, take my offer right away, or show me the property on my time. I learned very quickly that in life you can't let your pride get in the way of doing business.

I also believe that there is nothing wrong with partnering up with others when you get involved in real estate. Especially at the beginning if you don't have good credit or enough income to do it on your own. But like my big brother Rene Abreu has always told me, you should always partner up, never down. For example, if your partner has a $100,000 and you have $200,000, it's never gonna work. You should always pick a partner who is willing to come in with equal investment.

Last but not least, you should never become a deal junkie. I've seen many landlords being greedy and buying everything in sight just to prove that they have a lot of properties even when the deal isn't really a good one. Real estate is a numbers game. I truly believe that I am the king of making real estate numbers work. That's not me being cocky. That's just me being confident in the work that I do. I've put a lot of work into my business. Although I have lived the street life and have served time in prison, I am not and will never be ashamed of who I am or what I have been through. And neither should you. We all have a past. We've all done things in life that we know we shouldn't have. But none of us are perfect. Not even those who judge us are.

I'm not a licensed realtor and nobody in my family came from inheritance. I started from the bottom and made my way all the way up. I'm just a guy from the streets that's good at math like a million other people are out there in the world. I enjoy what I do. It's my life. Being a landlord will guarantee that the day I'm no longer here, that my daughter, nieces, and nephews will be taken care of for life. Rental income is forever. Like the saying goes, *"Without risk, there's no reward."* I live by those words.

I've learned to never take anything in my life for granted. Love those who love you. Never waste time on ignorance and always be productive in life. And to all my street guys out there and ex-felons coming home, always remember that if you can survive those two things, that you too can also be successful in real estate. Street smarts will always get you further in life than being book smart ever will. I'm living proof of that.

ACKNOWLEDGEMENTS

I would like to dedicate this book to the people that have helped me grow and mature into the person that I am today. I want to thank my wife Jennifer who's been with me through every stage of my life. It never mattered what situations I was in, she has always been the first to come to the rescue. You are my everything. To my daughter Taylor, I still remember the very first time I held you in my arms. You've changed my life in every unimaginable way that you can think of. You are the reason why I became the man that I am today. Everything that your mother and I do is all for you. I love you so much! To my brother Luchi, together we have enough crazy memories to last us a lifetime. You will always be my right hand man. To my parents, I know that we put you through hell while growing up, but we love you for always being there to support us. God has blessed me. You guys will never want for anything again. You are my world. To my grandparents, Ito and Ita, I want to thank you for showing me the definition of what real love means. You will always be the greatest grandparents.

To my mother-in law Daisy, thank you for always treating me like a son and accepting me as part of your family. You are all real examples of what family truly is.

Thank you to my big brother Rene Abreu for believing in me and also for all the advice and lessons that helped me take my business in real estate to the next level. Thank you to my attorney Joseph Conte for always having my back. You are the best in the business. Thank you to the first hard money lender Ildico Trien. You are a big part of my history.

Thank you to Johnny Marines, Fernando Hernandez, Danny Zu, Elyana Pacheco, Charles Tempio, Eric Rodriguez, Yanet Santana and Nitt Da Gritt. You are all great!

To all of the friends that I made while in prison, keep your head up and always think positive. We may have gone through hell, but life is long enough for us to learn to make better choices which can help us stay alive and free. I pray and hope that you all find the peace and happiness that you all deserve to have in your lives. Change the way you think and you will eventually find your purpose in life.

To the rest of my family and friends, I love y'all. Blessings to all of you!

A special thank you to the person who introduced me to the world. He saw what others didn't and without him, no one would know this story or even know my name. Thanks to DJ Envy. We have inspired many people to think differently and are helping our people become financially independent by building wealth through real estate.

CPSIA information can be obtained
at www.ICGtesting.com
Printed in the USA
BVHW040542230321
603180BV00006B/991

9 780578 847764